CONVERSATION GUIDE YALE

D0683405

ENGLISH-SPANISH

2nd edition
REVISED

EDITORIAL CANTABRICA, S. A. BILBAO

Traducción: Abilio Echeverría
Profesor de idiomas

Revisión: Carmen Aréchaga

Ilustraciones: Estudios B.C.

GUIAS PUBLICADAS

Español/Francés
Español/Inglés
Español/Alemán
Español/Italiano
Español/Euskara
Español/Portugués
Español/Catalán
Español/Arabe
Español/Holandés

English/Spanish
Deutsch/Spanisch
Français/Espagnol
Italiano/Spagnolo
Português/Espanhol
Arabe/Español
Nederlands/Spaans
Japanese/Spanish

GUIAS GASTRONOMICAS   TUTTO YALE

Manger en Espagne
Eating in Spain
Essen in Spanien

Las Plantas
Los Perros
Los Postres
El Bar en casa

Impreso en España
Printed in Spain

Depósito legal: BI. 392-94
I.S.B.N.: 84-221-0344-3

Edita:
© EDITORIAL CANTABRICA, S. A.
Nervión, 3 - 6.º
Telf. (94) 424 53 07
Fax (94) 423 19 84
48001 Bilbao-España

Impreso por: GRAFO, S. A. - Basauri - Bilbao

INDEX

INTRODUCTION

Here you have a Yale Guide, a booklet which wants to make itself useful and to be a handy travelling companion. Whether you have travelled or not, you will know how interesting and pleasing it is to be able to use the language spoken in the country you are visiting and how the Spanish people like to see you making an effort to approach them in their beautiful language. But up to which point can the YALE GUIDE help you? The answer depends upon your knowledge of the Spanish language.

IF YOU DO NOT KNOW ANY SPANISH AT ALL, this YALE will be an easy and entertaining guide to the language. It does not try to serve as a didactic text, but simply as a practical guide, capable of putting within your reach a complete collection of model phrases, which will not only enable you to make yourself understood in the most varied circumstances, but will also serve as a foundation for other similar ones. Do not hesitate to learn by heart several words and phrases daily. Practise them and always use them when the opportunity presents itself and you will be surprised to see with what speed and ease your knowledge widens. Do not be put off by the pronunciation barrier. It might turn out to be ridiculous asking for a glass of water by

5

mimicking, but never will it be so when asking for *oon vah'-soh deh ah'-goo-ah*, although the pronunciation might not fit to that which perhaps Salamanca University demands. At least you will avoid being served, after boastful mimicking, with tea with lemon.

IF YOU ALREADY HAVE SOME KNOWLEDGE OF SPANISH, this GUIDE will be of great help. A glance at it will suffice before entering a restaurant, a bank or a hairdresser's to remember which phrases are most appropriate in each case or which is the exact Spanish equivalent to that word which you have in mind. Always have this Guide within your reach; with it your knowledge of Spanish will widen to a much higher level to that which you had hoped to reach.

IF YOU MASTER SPANISH, the GUIDE will enable you to extend your knowledge to the maximum. On your frequent journeys or in your business you might perhaps deal with a faultless form of commercial terminology, but would you dare to be faced with a menu of typical dishes, or could you describe precisely to the shop assistant of the large stores the twinset which your wife asked you to take home for her? The YALE GUIDE will enable you to overcome these small gaps, enforcing your knowledge of the language to the utmost and making your stay in Spain twice as enjoyable.

6

FIGURED PRONUNCIATION

Spanish pronunciation is not at all difficult. It's really very easy due to the fact that Spanish words are pronounced exactly as they are written. The YALE GUIDE doesn't pretend to make you speak Spanish as a native, but to lend you a helping hand when you're travelling abroad. You'll be able to speak Spanish fluently enough to be understood everywhere without any trouble. We have achieved this by not using phonetic signs, symbols or letters which would take too long and perhaps not be as practical or effective. All you need is to read *with decision* the figured pronunciation of the sentence you want to pronounce and don't worry; the Spaniards will understand you perfectly.

A SYNOPSIS OF THE SPANISH GRAMMAR

1. THE ARTICLE

The definite article

Masculine: Sing. *El* (the); Pl. *Los* (the)
Feminine: Sing. *La* (the); Pl. *Las* (the)
Neuter: Sing. *Lo* (the).

When the article *el* comes after the prepositions *de* (of or from) or *a* (to), a contraction takes place: *de el = del*, *a el = al*.
To avoid the concurrence of two *a*'s we use the masculine form *el* before feminine nouns beginning with accented *a* or *ha*: *el agua* (the water), *el hacha* (the axe).
The neuter form *lo* is only used for abstract singular adjetives: *Lo eterno* (the eternal).

The indefinite article

Masculine: Sing. *Un* (a or an); Pl. *Unos* (some)
Feminine: Sing. *Una* (a or an); Pl. *Unas* (some)

To avoid the concurrence of two *a*'s we use the masculine form *un* before feminine nouns beginning with accented *a* or *ha*: *un águila* (an eagle), *un haya* (a beech-tree).

2. THE NOUN

Gender. The Spanish noun has no neuter gender. Every male animal is of the masculine gender; every female, of the feminine.

To inanimate objects an arbitrary gender is attributed: the names of things ending in *a*, *ad*, *ion* are for the most part feminine; those terminating in *o*, *i*, *o* are generally masculine.

Nouns ending in *o* change this *o* into *a* to form the feminine: *hijo* (son), *hija* (daughter); those terminating in a consonant add *a* for the feminine: *pastor* (shepherd), *pastora* (shepherdess).

Number. Nouns ending in an unaccented vowel add *s* to form the plural: *muchacho* (boy), *muchachos* (boys). Nouns terminating in an accented vowel or in a consonant form the plural by adding *es: rubí* (ruby), *rubíes* (rubies); *árbol* (tree), *árboles* (trees). Nouns ending in *z* change it into *c* when adding *es: juez* (judge), *jueces* (judges).

3. THE ADJECTIVE

The adjective, in Spanish, agrees with its noun in gender and number: «un niño *bueno*» (a *good* boy), «una niña *buena*» (a *good* girl); «niños *buenos*» (*good* boys), «niñas *buenas*» (*good* girls).

Gender. Adjectives ending in *o* are masculine and form the feminine by changing *o* into *a: malo-mala* (bad).

Adjectives not ending in *o* have only one termination for both genders: «un hombre *prudente*» (a prudent man), «una mujer *prudente*» (a prudent woman); «un objeto *trivial*» (a trivial object), «una cosa *trivial*» (a trivial thing). Exceptions: Adjectives ending in *on* or *an* and those, with a final consonant, derived from the names of countries add *a* to form the feminine, as *holgazán-holgazana* (idle), *español-española* (Spanish).

Number. Adjectives terminating in an unaccented vowel form their plural by adding s; those ending in an accented vowel or in a consonant add *es: blanco-blancos* (white), *baladí-baladíes* (trifling), *alemán-alemanes* (German).

Degrees of signification. The comparative of equality is formed with *tan ... como (as or so ... as)*; that of superiority, with *más ... que (more* or *-er than)*; that of inferiority, with *menos ... que (less ... than)*.

The relative superlative -formed in English with *-est* or *the most-* is rendered by prefixing the definite article to the Spanish comparative: *el más rico* (the richest), *la más hermosa* (the most beautiful). The absolute superlative —formed in English with *very*— is rendered by prefixing the adverb *muy* to the adjective or by adding to it the termination *-ísimo: muy docto* or *doctísimo* (very learned). The following adjectives have *irregular* degrees of comparison: *bueno* (good), *mejor* (better), *óptimo* (very good); *malo* (bad), *peor* (worst), *pésimo* (very bad); *grande* (great, large), *mayor* (greater, larger), *máximo* (very great, very large); *pequeño* (little, small), *menor* (less, smaller), *mínimo* (very little, very small).

4. THE PRONOUNS

There are six kinds: Personal, Demonstrative, Possessive, Interrogative, Relative and Indefinite pronouns. When followed by a noun, the demonstrative, possessive, interrogative and indefinite pronouns are considered to be adjectives.

PERSONAL PRONOUNS

	Sing.	Plur.
1st Person.	Yo, me, mí (I, me)	Nosotros, nos (We, us)
2nd Person.	Tú, te, ti (You)	Vosotros, os (You)
	Usted, le	Ustedes, les

3rd Person.	El, le, lo	(He, him)	Ellos, les, los	(They,
	Ella, le, la	(She, her)	Ellas, les, las	them)
	Ello, lo	(It)		

Mí, ti are always preceded by prepositions.

Me, te, le, lo, la, las, les are never placed after prepositions and precede the verb in the Indicative and Subjunctive moods, as well as in the Imperative when negatively employed.

The only reflexive form is *se* (3rd Person, sing. and plur.); the other persons employ the objective form of the pronoun as their reflexive: *me, te, nos, os*.

DEMONSTRATIVE PRONOUNS

Sing.			Plur.	
Masc.	Fem.	Neut.	Masc.	Fem.
Este,	ésta,	esto:	this	Estos,	éstas:	these
Ese,	ésa,	eso:	that	Esos,	ésas:	those
Aquél,	aquélla,	aquello:	that	Aquéllos,	aquéllas:	those

These pronouns, when followed by a noun, are adjectives.

POSSESSIVE PRONOUNS

Sing.			Plur.		
Masc.	Fem.		Masc.	Fem.	
Mío	mía:	mine	Míos	mías:	mine
Tuyo	tuya:	yours	Tuyos	tuyas:	yours
Suyo	suya:	his, hers, its	Suyos	suyas:	his, hers, its
Nuestro	nuestra:	ours	Nuestros	nuestras:	ours
Vuestro	vuestra:	yours	Vuestros	vuestras:	yours
Suyo	suya:	theirs	Suyos	suyas:	theirs

When used as pronouns, they are generally preceded by the definite article.

When employed as adjectives, they assume *short* forms, as follows:

Sing.	Plur.	
mi	mis:	my
tu	tus:	your
su	sus:	his, her, its
nuestro, -a;	-os, -as:	our
vuestro, -a;	-os, -as:	your
su	sus:	their

INTERROGATIVE PRONOUNS

Sing.	Plur.	
¿Quién?	¿Quiénes?:	Who?
¿Cuál?	¿Cuáles?	Which?
¿Qué?:		What?

RELATIVE PRONOUNS

Sing.	Plur.	
Quien	Quienes	Who
Cuyo, -a	Cuyos, -as:	Whose
El, la cual	Los, las cuales:	Who, Which
Que:		Who, Which, That

INDEFINITE PRONOUNS

Sing.	Plur.	
Alguno, -a	Algunos, -as:	Some, any
Alguien:		Somebody, anybody
Ninguno, -a	Ningunos, -as:	None, nobody
Nadie:		Nobody
Cualquiera	Cualesquiera:	Whoever, whichever, whatever
Quienquiera	Quienesquiera:	Whoever
	Ambos:	Both
Otro, -a	Otros, -as:	Other, another
Mismo, -a	Mismos, -as	Same
Todo el mundo		Everyone, everybody
Todo, -a	Todos, -as:	All
Tal	Tales:	Such
Algo		Something, Anything
Nada		Nothing
Cualquier cosa		Everything

5. THE VERB

Spanish verbs are classed into three conjugations according to the termination of the infinitive mood: 1st, verbs ending in *-ar*, as *amar* (to love); 2nd, verbs ending in *-er*, as *temer* (to fear); 3rd, verbs ending in *-ir*, as *batir* (to beat).

TABLE OF THE TERMINATIONS OF ALL THE REGULAR VERBS IN THE THREE CONJUGATIONS

(SIMPLE TENSES)

INDICATIVE MOOD

Present

-o	-o	-o
-as	-es	-es
-a	-e	-e
-amos	-emos	-imos
-áis	-éis	-ís
-an	-en	-en

Imperfect

-aba	-ía	-ía
-abas	-ías	-ías
-aba	-ía	-ía
-ábamos	-íamos	-íamos
-abais	-íais	-íais
-aban	-ían	-ían

Preterite

-é	-í	-í
-aste	-iste	-iste
-ó	-ió	-ió
-amos	-imos	-imos
-asteis	-isteis	-isteis
-aron	-ieron	-ieron

Future

-aré	-eré	-iré
-arás	-erás	-irás
-ará	-erá	-irá
-aremos	-eremos	-iremos
-aréis	-eréis	-iréis
-arán	-erán	-irán

IMPERATIVE MOOD

-	-	-
-a	-e	-e
-e	-a	-a
-emos	-amos	-amos
-ad	-ed	-id
-en	-an	-an

SUBJUNCTIVE MOOD

Present

-e	-a	-a
-es	-as	-as
-e	-a	-a
-emos	-amos	-amos
-éis	-áis	-áis
-en	-an	-an

Imperfect
(First termination)

-ara	-iera	-iera
-aras	-ieras	-ieras
-ara	-iera	-iera
-áramos	-iéramos	-iéramos
-arais	-ierais	-ierais
-aran	-ieran	-ieran

14

Imperfect
(Second termination)

-ase	-iese	-iese
-ases	-ieses	-ieses
-ase	-iese	-iese
-ásemos	-iésemos	-iésemos
-aseis	-ieseis	-ieseis
-asen	-iesen	-iesen

Future

-are	-iere	-iere
-ares	-ieres	-ieres
-are	-iere	-iere
-áremos	-iéremos	-iéremos
-areis	-iereis	-iereis
-aren	-ieren	-ieren

CONDITIONAL MOOD

-aría	-ería	-iría
-arías	-erías	-irías
-aría	-ería	iría
-aríamos	-eríamos	-iríamos
-aríais	-eríais	-iríais
-arían	-erían	-irían

INFINITIVE

-ar	-er	-ir

GERUND

-ando	-iendo	-iendo

PAST PART.

-ado	-ido	-ido

Compound tenses are formed by adding to the respective forms of the auxiliary verb *haber* (to have) the past participle of the verb that is conjugated: *Yo he amado* (I have loved).

The pasive voice is formed by adding to the respective forms of the auxiliary verb *ser* (to be) the past participle of the verb that is conjugated: *Yo soy amado* (I am loved).

THE AUXILIARY VERBS *HABER* AND *SER*

INDICATIVE MOOD

Present

He	I have	Soy	I am
Has	you have	Eres	you are
Ha	he has	Es	he is
Hemos	we have	Somos	we are
Habéis	you have	Sois	you are
Han	they have	Son	they are

Imperfect

Había	I had	Era	I was
Habías	you had	Eras	you were
Había	he had	Era	he was
Habíamos	we had	Eramos	we were
Habíais	you had	Erais	you were
Habían	they had	Eran	they were

Preterite

Hube	I had	Fuí	I was
Hubiste	you had	Fuiste	you were
Hubo	he had	Fue	he was
Hubimos	we had	Fuimos	we were
Hubisteis	you had	Fuisteis	you were
Hubieron	they had	Fueron	they were

Future

Habré	I shall have	Seré	I shall be
Habrás	you will have	Serás	you will be
Habrá	he will have	Será	he will be
Habremos	we shall have	Seremos	we shall be
Habréis	you will have	Seréis	you will be
Habrán	they will have	Serán	they will be

IMPERATIVE MOOD

He tú	have	Se tú	be
Haya usted	have	Sea usted	be
Habed vosotros	have	Sed vosotros	be
Hayan ustedes	have	Sean ustedes	be

SUBJUNCTIVE MOOD

Present

Haya	that I have	Sea.	if I be
Hayas	that you have	Seas	if you be
Haya	that he have	Sea	if he be
Hayamos	that we have	Seamos	if we be
Hayáis	that you have	Seáis	if you be
Hayan	that they have	Sean	if they be

Imperfect
(First termination)

Hubiera	that I had	Fuera	if I were
Hubieras	that you had	Fueras	if you were
Hubiera	that he had	Fuera	if he were
Hubiéramos	that we had	Fuéramos	if we were
Hubierais	that you had	Fuerais	if you were
Hubieran	that they had	Fueran	if they were

Imperfect
(Second termination)

Hubiese	that I had	Fuese	if I were
Hubieses	that you had	Fueses	if you were
Hubiese	that he had	Fuese	if he were
Hubiésemos	that we had	Fuésemos	if we were
Hubieseis	that you had	Fueseis	if you were
Hubiesen	that they had	Fuesen	if they were

17

CONDITIONAL MOOD

Habría	I should have	Sería	I should be
Habrías	you would have	Serías	you would be
Habría	he would have	Sería	he would be
Habríamos	we should have	Seríamos	we should be
Habríais	you would have	Seríais	you would be
Habrían	they would have	Serían	they would be

INFINITIVE MOOD
Present

Haber	to have	Ser	to be

Gerund

Habiendo	having	Siendo	being

Past participle

Habido	had	Sido	been

The *negative conjugation* is rendered by placing the adverb *no* before the verb: *Yo no amo* (I do not love).

The *interrogative conjugation* is rendered by placing the subject after the verb: *¿ Vino tu amigo?* (Did your friend come?).

6. THE ADVERB

English adverbs ending in -*ly* are formed from the respective adjective by the addition of the termination -*mente: fácil-fácilmente* (easy-easily).

In compound tenses, the adverb cannot take its place between the auxiliary and the participle, as in English: *El ha venido siempre conmigo* (He has always come with me). Adverbs form the comparative like the adjectives *(fácilmente, más fácilmente, menos fácilmente)* and admit the superlative (facilísimamente).

In Spanish, as in English, there are seven kinds of adverbs:

1. **of manner**

well	bien
badly	mal
fast	de prisa
happily	felizmente
quickly	rápidamente

and most of the adverbs ended in *-mente;*

2. **of place**

here	aquí
there	ahí, allí
up	arriba
down	abajo
near	cerca
far	lejos
everywhere	en todas partes;

3. **of time**

now	ahora
then	entonces
soon	pronto
still	todavía
yet	aún
today	hoy
yesterday	ayer
to-morrow	mañana

4. **of frequency**

twice	dos veces
often	frecuentemente
never	nunca
ever	alguna vez
always	siempre
occasionally	a veces

5. **of degree**

very	muy
fairly	bastante
rather	más bien

quite	totalmente
too	demasiado
hardly	apenas;

6. **interrogative**

when?	¿cuándo?
where?	¿dónde?
why?	¿por qué?

7. **relative**

| where | donde |
| why | por que, por lo que |

7. PREPOSITIONS

Above = sobre, encima de	For = para
According = según	From = de, desde
After = después, detrás de	In = en, dentro de
Against = contra	Into = a dentro de
Among = entre	Of = de
At = en, junto a	On = sobre
Before = delante de	Over = encima de
Behind = detrás de	Since = desde hace
Below = debajo de	Through = a través de
Beside = al lado de	Till = hasta
Between = entre	To = a, hacia
By = por	Towards = hacia
Down = abajo de	With = con
During = durante	Without = sin

COMMON PHRASES

Here you have at your disposal various phrases and expressions which often come up in a conversation. Try to remember them, choose the appropriate moment to make use of them and you yourself will be surprised of your rapid progress in simple conversations.

GREETINGS

Good morning
Buenos días
Boo-eh'-nohs dee'-as

Good evening
Buenas tardes
Boo-eh'-nas tar'-des

Good night
Buenas noches
Boo-eh'-nas nau'-ches

How do you do?
¿Qué hay?
¿Qué tal?
Keh' ah'-ee?
Keh'tahl?

How are you?
¿Cómo está usted?
Cau'-moh es-tah' oos-ted'?

Very well, thank you
Muy bien, gracias
Moo'-e be-en', grah'-the-as

And your family?
¿Y su familia?
Ee soo fah-mee'-le-ah?

All right
Están bien
Es-tahn' be-en'

See you tomorrow
Hasta mañana
As'-tah mah-nyah'-nah

Good bye
Hasta la vista
As'-tah lah vee's-tah

See you soon
Hasta pronto
As'tah praun'-toh

QUESTIONS

Do you speak Spanish?
¿Habla usted español?
ah'-blah oos-ted' es-pah-nyaul'?

Do you understand?
¿Comprende usted?
Caum-pren'-deh oos'-ted'?

What did you say?
¿Cómo ha dicho?
Cau'-moh ah dee'-choh?

What are you saying?
¿Qué dice usted?
Keh'dee'-theh oos-ted'?

What do you say?
¿Cómo dice?
Cau'-moh dee'-theh?

Who is it?
¿Quién es?
Ke-en'es?

What is that?
¿Qué es eso?
Keh' es eh'-soh?

Where are you going?
¿Dónde va usted?
Daun'-deh vah oos-ted'?

What do you want?
¿Qué quiere usted?
Keh' ke-eh'-reh oos-ted'?

Are you sure?
¿Está usted seguro?
Es-tah' oos-ted' seh-goo'-roh?

Really?
¿De veras?
Deh veh'-ras?

How much?
¿Cuánto?
Coo-ahn'-toh?

How many?
¿Cuántos?
Coo-ahn'-tohs?

Here or there?
¿Aquí o allá?
Ah-kee' oh ah-lyah'?

Why?
¿Por qué?
Paur keh'?

ASSERTIONS

Yes
Sí
See

O.K. (All right)
De acuerdo
Deh ah-coo-er'-doh

It is true
Es verdad
Es ver-dahd'

Perhaps, maybe
Quizá
Ke-thah'

As you like
Como usted quiera
Cau'-moh oos-ted' ke-eh'-rah

As soon as you like
Cuando usted guste
Coo-ahn'-doh oos-ted' goos'-teh

You are right
Tiene usted razón
Ti-eh'-neh oos-ted' rah-thaun'

I understand
Entiendo
En-te-en'-doh

NEGATIONS

No
No
No

Not at all
En absoluto
En ab-sau-loo'-toh

Never
Nunca
Noon'-cah

Nobody, none
Nadie
Nah'-de-eh

I do not know
No sé
No seh

I beg your pardon
Lo siento
Loh se-en'-toh

I do not understand	I do not think so	You are wrong
No entiendo	No creo	Está usted confundido
No en-te-en'-doh	*No creh'-oh*	*Es-tah' oos-ted' caun-foon-dee'-doh*

It is wrong	Nothing	It is impossible
Es falso	Nada	Es imposible
Es fahl'-soh	*Nah'-dah*	*Es im-pau-see'-bleh*

INTRODUCTIONS

Let me introduce you Mr...	Glad to see you	My name is
Le presento al Sr...	Mucho gusto	Me llamo
Leh preh-sen'-toh ahl seh-nyaur'...	*Moo'-choh goos'-toh*	*Meh lyah'-moh*

COMPLIMENTS

Thank you	Thank you very much	Please
Gracias	Muchas gracias	Por favor
Grah'-the-as	*Moo'-chas grah'-the-as*	*Paur fah-vaur'*

I beg you	With pleasure	Cheers
Se lo ruego	Con mucho gusto	A su salud
Seh lau roo-eh'-goh	*Caun moo'-choh goos'-toh*	*Ah soo sah-lood'*

Sit down, please	Excuse me	I beg your pardon
Siéntese, por favor	Dispense	Perdón
Se-en'-teh-seh, paur fah-vaur'	*Dis-pen'-seh*	*Per-daun'*

You are very kind
Es usted muy amable
Es oos-ted' moo'-e ah'mah'-bleh

EXCLAMATIONS

What a pretty thing!	Wonderful!	What a pleasure
¡Qué cosa más bonita!	¡Maravilloso!	¡Qué gusto!
Keh' cau'-sah mas bau-nee'-tah!	*Mah-rah-ve-lyau'-soh!*	*Keh'goos'-toh!*

What a luck!	That is funny	What a pity!
¡Qué suerte!	Es curioso	¡Qué lástima!
Keh'soo-er'-teh!	*Es coo-re-au'-soh!*	*Keh' las'-te-mah!*

What a nuisance!	What a nonsense!	What a shame!
¡Qué fastidio!	¡Qué tontería!	¡Qué vergüenza!
Keh'fas-tee'-de-oh!	*Keh' taun-teh-ree'-ah!*	*Keh' ver-goo-en'-thah!*

25

ORDERS

Speak slowly	**Hurry up, please**	**The bill!**
Hable más despacio	Por favor, dese prisa	¡La cuenta!
Ah'-bleh mas' des-pah'-the-oh	*Paur fah-vaur', deh'-seh pree'-sah*	*Lah coo-en'-tah!*
Waiter	**Come here!**	**Give me!**
¡Camarero!	¡Venga aquí!	¡Deme!
Cah-mah-reh'-roh!	*Ven'-gah ah'kee'!*	*Deh'-meh!*
Get out!	**Listen!**	**Silence**
¡Salga!	¡Escuche!	Silencio
Sahl'-gah!	*Es-coo'-cheh!*	*Se-len'-the-oh*
Help!		
¡Socorro!		
Sau-caur'-roh!		

WORDS FREQUENTLY USED

Moreover	**Ahead**	**Around**
Además	Adelante	Alrededor de
Ah-deh-mas'	*Ah-deh-lahn'-teh*	*Ahl-reh-deh-daur' deh*
Sometimes	**There**	**Before**
Algunas veces	Allí	Antes de
Ahl-goo'-nas veh'-thes	*Ah-lyee'*	*Ahn'-tes deh*
Scarcely	**Here**	**Up**
Apenas	Aquí	Arriba
Ah-peh'-nas	*Ah-kee'*	*Ar-ree'-bah*

Backwards	**Well**	**Almost**
Atrás	Bien	Casi
Ah-tras'	*Be-en'*	*Cah'-see*
Near	**How?**	**Against**
Cerca de	¿Cómo?	Contra
Ther'-cah deh	*Kau-moh?*	*Caun'-trah*
When?	**How much?**	**How many?**
¿Cuándo?	¿Cuánto?	¿Cuántos?
Coo-ahn'-do?	*Coo-ahn'-toh?*	*Coo-ahn'-tohs?*
Under	**In front of**	**In**
Debajo de	Delante de	Dentro de
Deh-bah'-hoh deh	*Deh-lahn'-teh deh*	*Den'troh deh*
Too much	**Too many**	**From**
Demasiado	Demasiados	Desde
Deh-mah-se-ah'-doh	*Deh-mah-se-ah'-dohs*	*Des'-deh*
Slowly	**After**	**Behind**
Despacio	Después de	Detrás
Des-pah'-the-oh	*Des'-poo-es' deh*	*Deh-tras'*
Where?	**During**	**In**
¿Dónde?	Durante	En
Daun' deh?	*Doo-rahn'-teh*	*Ehn*
On	**Opposite**	**Elsewhere**
Encima	En frente	En otra parte
En-thee'-mah	*En fren'-teh*	*En au'-trah par'-teh*
Forthwith	**Everywhere**	**Then**
En seguida	En todas partes	Entonces
En seh-ghee'-dah	*En tau'-das par'-tes*	*En-taun'-thes*
Except	**Out**	**Towards**
Excepto	Fuera de	Hacia
Ex-thep'toh	*Foo-eh'-rah deh*	*Ah'-the-ah*

27

Till	**Far**	**More**
Hasta	Lejos	Más
As'-tah	*Leh'-hohs*	*Mas'*

Less	**Much**	**Many**
Menos	Mucho	Muchos
Meh'-nohs	*Moo'-choh*	*Moo'-chohs*

Very	**For**	**Because**
Muy	Para	Porque
Moo'-e	*Pah'-rah*	*Paur'-keh*

Why?	**According to**	**Soon**
¿Por qué?	Según	Pronto
Paur keh'?	*Seh-goon'*	*Praun'-toh*

Fast	**Only**	**Always**
Rápido	Sólo	Siempre
Rah'-pe-doh	*Sau'-loh*	*Se-em'-preh*

Without	**Soon**	**Too**
Sin	Temprano	También
Seen	*Tem-prah'-noh*	*Tahm-be-en'*

Yet, still	**A little**	**And**
Todavía	Un poco	Y
Tau-dah-vee'-ah	*Oon pau'-coh*	*Ee*

PUBLIC NOTICES

Caution
Cuidado
Coo-e-dah'-doh

Closed
Cerrado
Ther-rah'-doh

Danger
Peligro
Peh-lee'-groh

Elevator
Ascensor
As-then-saur'

Entrance
Entrada
En-trah'-dah

Exit
Salida
Sah-lee'-dah

For hire (rent)
Se alquila
Seh ahl-kee'-lah

For sale
Se vende
Seh ven'-deh

Free
Libre
Lee'-breh

High tension wires
Cables de alta tensión
Cah'-bles deh ahl'-tah ten-se-aun'

Keep off the grass
Prohibido pisar el césped
Prau-e-bee'-doh pe-sar' el thes'-ped

Keep out
Prohibido el paso
Prau-e-bee'-doh el pah'-soh

29

Ladies
Señoras
Seh-nyau'-ras

Lavatory
Lavabos
Lah-vah'-bohs

Lift
Ascensor
As-then-saur'

Men
Caballeros
Cah-bah-lyeh'-rohs

No admittance
Se prohibe la entrada
Seh prau-ee'-beh lah en-trah'-dah

No smoking
Se prohibe fumar
Seh prau-ee'-beh foo-mar'

Engaged
Ocupado
Au-coo-pah'-doh

Open
Abierto
Ah-be-er'-toh

Silence
Silencio
Se-len'-the-oh

Stick no bills
Prohibido fijar carteles
Prau-e-bee'-doh fe-har' cahr-teh'-les

To the right (left)
A la derecha (izquierda)
Ah lah deh-reh'-chah (ith-ke-er'-dah)

Wet paint
Cuidado con la pintura
Coo-e-dah'-doh caun lah pin-too'-rah

Pull
Tirar
Te-rar'

Push
Empujar
Em-poo-har'

Private
Privado
Pre-vah'-doh

Beware of...
Atención al...
Ah-ten-the-aun' ahl...

Men at work
Obras
Au'-bras

Ring the bell
Llame al timbre
Lyah'-meh ahl teem'-breh

TRAFFIC

Crossroads

Cruce
Croo'-theh

Danger

Peligro
Peh-lee'-groh

Dangerous curve

Curva peligrosa
Coor'-vah peh-le-grau'-sah

Dead end

Calle sin salida
Cah'-lyeh seen sah-lee'-dah

Diversion

Desviación
Des-ve-ah-the-aun'

Level crossing

Paso a nivel
Pah'-soh ah ne-vel'

Narrow

Estrecho
Es-treh'-choh

One way

Dirección única
De-rec-the-aun' oo'-ne-cah

Motorway

Autopista
Ah-oo-tau-pees'-tah

School

Escuela

Es-coo-eh'-lah

Slow down

Despacio

Des-pah'-the-oh

Speed limit

Velocidad limitada
Veh-lau-the-dahd' le-me-tah'-dah

NUMBERS

1. Uno. *Oo'-noh*
2. Dos. *Daus*
3. Tres. *Tres*
4. Cuatro. *Coo-ah'-troh*
5. Cinco. *Theen'-coh*
6. Seis. *Seh'-ees*
7. Siete. *Se-eh'-teh*
8. Ocho. *Au'-choh*
9. Nueve. *Noo-eh'-veh*
10. Diez. *De-eht'*

11. Once. *Aun'-theh*
12. Doce. *Dau'-theh*
13. Trece. *Treh'-theh*
14. Catorce. *Cah-taur'-theh*
15. Quince. *Keen'-theh*
16. Dieciséis. *De-eh-the-seh'-ees*
17. Diecisiete. *De-eh-the-se-eh'-teh*
18. Dieciocho. *De-eh-the-au'-choh*
19. Diecinueve. *De-eh-the-noo-eh'-veh*
20. Veinte. *Veh'-in-teh*

21. Veintiuno. *Veh-in-te-oo'-noh*
22. Veintidós. *Veh-in-te-daus'*
23. Veintitrés. *Veh-in-te-tres'*
24. Veinticuatro. *Veh-in-te-coo-ah'-troh*

30. Treinta. *Treh'-in-tah*
40. Cuarenta. *Coo-ah-ren'-tah*
50. Cincuenta. *Thin-coo-en'-tah*
60. Sesenta. *Seh-sen'-tah*
70. Setenta. *Seh-ten'-tah*
80. Ochenta. *Au-chen' tah*
90. Noventa. *Nau-ven'-tah*

100.	Cien. *The-en'*
200.	Doscientos. *Daus-the-en'-tohs*
300.	Trescientos. *Trehs-the-en'-tohs*
400.	Cuatrocientos. *Coo-ah-troh-the-en'-tohs*
500.	Quinientos. *Ke-ne-en'-tohs*
600.	Sciscientos. *Seh-ees-the-en'-tohs*
700.	Setecientos. *Seh-teh-the-en'-tohs*
800.	Ochocientos. *Au-choh-the-en'-tohs*
900.	Novecientos. *Nau-veh-the-en'-tohs*
1.000.	Mil. *Meel*
10.000.	Diez mil. *De-eth' meel*
1.000.000.	Un millón. *Oon mil-lyaun'*

1.º.	Primero. *Pre-meh'-roh*
2.º.	Segundo. *Seh-goon'-doh*
3.º.	Tercero. *Ter-theh'-roh*
4.º.	Cuarto. *Coo-ar'-toh*
5.º.	Quinto. *Keen'-toh*
6.º.	Sexto. *Sex'-toh*
7.º.	Séptimo. *Sep'-te-moh*
8.º.	Octavo. *Auc-tah'-voh*
9.º.	Noveno. *Nau-veh'-noh*
10.º.	Décimo. *Deh'-the-moh*

1/2.	Medio. *Meh'-de-oh*
1/3.	Un tercio. *Oon ter'-the-oh*
1/4.	Un cuarto. *Oon coo-ar'-toh*
1/5.	Un quinto. *Oon keen'-toh*
1/6.	Un sexto. *Oon sex'-toh*
1/7.	Un séptimo. *Oon sep'-te-moh*
1/8.	Un octavo. *Oon auc-tah'-voh*
1/9.	Un noveno. *Oon nau-veh'-noh*
1/10.	Un décimo. *Oon deh'-the-moh*

TRAVELLING

Travelling is certainly enjoyable, but you ought to be prepared for small incidents which could turn into unpleasant problems. If you are going in your own car, with a road map, which is indeed a must, do not forget the YALE Guide, which will be able to help you out when in trouble if you are as unfortunate as to have a breakdown. In the same way, it will help you to go through the customs, to buy a ticket for the means of transport which you have chosen and to know from which platform the train leaves or from which runway your plane takes off. With this Guide you will also be able to make your self understood to a taxidriver or a bus conductor, who most likely does not have any knowledge of English.

CUSTOMS-HOUSE

Customs-house	**Name**	**Surname**
Aduana	Nombre	Apellido
Ah-doo-ah'-nah	*Naum'-breh*	*Ah-peh-lyee'-doh*
Documentation	**Luggage**	**Passport**
Documentación	Equipaje	Pasaporte
Dau-coo-men-tah-the-aun'	*Eh-ke-pah'-heh*	*Pah-sah-paur'-teh*

International driving licence
Permiso internacional de conducir
Pehr-mee'-soh in-tehr-nah-the-au-nahl' deh caun-doo-theer'

Present, gift   Customs duties
Regalo   Derechos de aduana
Reh-gah'-loh   *Deh-reh'-chohs deh ah-doo-ah'-nah*

Exchange office
Oficina de cambio
Au-fe-thee' nah deh cahm'-be-oh

Passport, please
Por favor, su pasaporte
Paur fah-vaur', soo pah-sah-paur'-teh

Show me your papers and the health certificate
Muéstreme su documentación y el certificado médico
Moo-es'-treh-meh soo dau-coo-men-tah-the-aun' ee el ther-te-fe-cah'-doh meh'-de-coh

Have you anything to declare?
¿Tiene usted algo que declarar?
Te-eh'-neh oos-ted' ahl'-goh keh deh-clah-rahr'?

Nothing
Nada
Nah'-dah

I have some bottles of whisky and cigarettes
Llevo algunas botellas de whisky y cigarrillos
Lyeh'-voh ahl-goo'-nas bau-teh'-lyas deh goo-is'-ke ee the-gar-ree'-lyohs

Open your bags
Abra sus maletas
Ah'-brah soos mah-leh'-tas

35

Must I pay for these presents?
¿Debo pagar por estos regalos?
Deh'-boh pah-gar'paur es'-tohs reh-gah'-lohs?

What have you in these parcels?
¿Qué hay en estos paquetes?
Keh ah'-ee en es'-tohs pah-keh'-tes?

Personal effects and kitchen utensils
Objetos de uso personal y artículos de cocina
Aub-heh'-tohs deh oo'-soh pehr-sau-nahl' ee ar-tee'-coo-lohs deh cau-thee'-nah

May I close my bags?
¿Puedo cerrar mis maletas?
Poo-eh'-doh ther-rar' mees mah-leh'-tas?

How much must I pay?
¿Cuánto debo pagar?
Coo-ahn'-toh deh'-boh pah-gar'?

Is everything O.K.?
¿Está todo en orden?
Es-tah' tau'-do en aur'-den?

Where is the exchange office?
¿Dónde está la oficina de cambio?
Daun'-deh es-tah'lah au-fe-thee'-nah deh cahm'-be-oh?

What is the rate for the peseta?
¿Cuál es la cotización de la peseta?
Coo-ahl' es lah cau-te-tha-the-aun' deh lah peh-seh'-tah?

Can you change ... pesetas?
¿Puede cambiarme ... pesetas?
Poo-eh'-deh cahm-be-ar'-meh ... peh-seh'-tas?

Where can I find a taxi?
¿Dónde puedo encontrar un taxi?
Daun'-deh poo-eh'-doh en-caun-trar'oon tak'-se?

THE SHIP

Port	**Quay**	**Cabin**
Puerto	Muelle	Camarote
Poo-er'-toh	*Moo-eh'-lyeh*	*Cah-mah-rau'-teh*

Bow	**Stern**	**Hold**
Proa	Popa	Bodega
Prau'-ah	*Pau'-pah*	*Bau-deh'-gah*

Port side	**Starboard side**	**Rudder**
Babor	Estribor	Timón
Bah-baur'	*Es-tre-baur'*	*Te-maun'*

Deck	**Captain**	**Pilot**
Cubierta	Capitán	Piloto
Coo-be-er'-tah	*Cah-pe-tahn'*	*Pe-lau'-toh*

Seaman, sailor	Crossing	To call (at a port)
Marinero	Travesía	Hacer escala
Mah-re-neh'-roh	*Trah-veh-see'-ah*	*Ah-ther' es-cah'-lah*

To come alongside	To heave up anchor	Deck chair
Atracar	Levar anclas	Hamaca
Ah-trah-car'	*Leh-var' ahn'-clas*	*Ah-mah'-cah*

On what day (at what time) does the ship sail for...?

¿Qué día (a qué hora) sale el barco para...?

Keh' dee'-ah (ah keh' au'-rah) sah'-leh el bar'-coh pah'-rah...?

I want a passage for...

Desearía un pasaje para...

Deh-seh-ah-ree'-ah oon pah-sah'-heh pah'-rah...

Give me a first class cabin

Deme un camarote de primera clase

Deh'-meh oon cah-mah-rau'-teh deh pre-meh'-rah cla'-seh

You must be at the port two hours before sailing

Debe estar en el puerto dos horas antes de la salida

Deh'-beh es-tar' en el poo-er'-toh daus au'-ras ahn'-tes deh lah sah-lee'-dah

From what quay does the ship sail?

¿De qué muelle sale el barco?

Deh keh' moo-eh'-lyeh sah'-leh el bar'-co?

Where is my cabin?

¿Dónde está mi camarote?

Daun'-deh es-tah' me cah-mah-rau'-teh?

Your cabin is forward
Su camarote está situado a proa
Soo cah-mah-rau'-teh es-tah' se-too-ah'-doh ah prau'-ah

This way, mind your head!
Por aquí, ¡cuidado con la cabeza!
Paur ah-kee', coo-e-dah'-doh caun lah cah-beh'-thah!

These parcels must travel in the baggage hold
Estos bultos deben ir en la bodega
Es'-tohs bool'-tohs deh'-ben eer en lah bau-deh'-gah

How many times shall we call before...?
¿Cuántas escalas haremos antes de llegar a...?
Coo-ahn'-tas es-cah'-las ah-reh'-mohs ahn'-tes deh lye-gar'ah....?

The ship will call in...
El barco atracará en los puertos de...
El bar'-coh ah-trah-cah-rah' en lohs poor-er'-tohs deh...

Look, we are about to heave up anchors
¡Atención! El barco va a levar anclas
Ah-ten-the-aun'! El bar'-coh vah ah leh-var' ahn'-clas

Hold tight!
¡Agárrense bien!
Ah-gar'-ren-seh be-en'!

I am seasick
Me mareo
Meh mah-reh'-oh

Have you got pills for seasickness?
¿Tiene píldoras contra el mareo?
Te-eh'-neh peel'-dau-ras caun'-trah el mah-reh'-oh?

Where is the bar?
¿Dónde está el bar?
Daun'-deh es-tah' el bar?

It is not open before ten
No abre hasta las diez
Nau ah'-breh as'-tah las de-eth'

Waiter, will you please get me a deck chair?
Camarero, ¿puede proporcionarme una hamaca
por favor?
Cah-mah-reh'-roh, poo-eh'-deh prau-paur-the-au-nar'-me oo'-nah ah-mah'-cah, paur fah-vaur'?

We are coming into the harbour
Entramos ya en el puerto
En-trah'-mohs yah en el poo-er'-toh

Will it be long before going ashore?
¿Tardaremos en desembarcar?
Tar-dah-reh'-mohs en deh-sehm-bar-car'?

Please put my baggage on the quay
Sírvase bajar mis maletas al muelle
Seer'-vah-seh bah-har' mees mah-leh'-tas ahl moo-eh'-lyeh

Is there a nurse on board?
¿Hay enfermera a bordo?
Ah'ee en-fer-meh'rah ah baur'doh?

Please, I would like her to come
Por favor, quisiera que viniese
Paur fah-vaur', ke-se-eh'-rah keh ve-ne-eh'-seh

Where is the infirmary?
¿Dónde está la enfermería?
Daun'-deh es-tah' lah en-fer-meh-ree'-ah?

THE TRAIN

Station
La estación
Lah es-ta-the-aun'

Platform
El andén
El ahn-den'

Tracks
Las vías
Las vee'-as

Locomotive
Locomotora
Lau-cau-mau-tau'-rah

Window
Ventanilla
Ven-tah-nee'-lyah

Inspector
Revisor
Reh-ve-saur'

Porter
Mozo
Mau'-thoh

Traveller
Viajero
Ve-ah-heh'-roh

Trunk
Baúl
Bah-ool'

Bag
Maleta
Mah-leh'-tah

Handbag
Maletín
Mah-leh-teen'

Baggage
Equipaje
Eh-ke-pah'-heh

41

Ticket	Single (one way)	Return (round trip)
Billete	Ida	Ida y vuelta
Be-lyeh'-teh	*Ee'-dah*	*Ee'-dah ee voo-el'-tah*

1st class	2nd class	Left luggage office
Primera	Segunda	Consigna
Pree-meh'-rah	*Seh-goon'-dah*	*Caun-seeg'-nah*

Sleeping-car	Dining car
Coche cama	Coche restaurante
Cau'-cheh cah'-mah	*Cau'-cheh res-tah-oo-rahn'-teh*

Where is the ticket office?
¿Dónde está la taquilla?
Daun'-deh es-tah' lah tah-kee'-lyah?

What is the fare to...?
¿Cuál es el precio de un billete para...?
Coo-ahl' es el preh'-the-oh deh oon be-lyeh'-teh pah-rah...?

There is no train to-day
Hoy no hay tren
Au'-ee no ah'-ee trehn

A ticket to Valladolid
Un billete para Valladolid
Oon be-lyeh'-teh pah'-rah vah-lyah-do-leed'

By which train?
¿Para qué tren?
Pah'-rah keh' tren?

Is there a special fare for children?
¿Hay tarifa reducida para niños?
Ah'-ee tah-ree'-fah reh-doo-thee'-dah pah-rah nee'-nyohs?

How much is it?
¿Cuánto es?
Coo-ahn-toh es?

I want my baggage registered (checked)
Quiero facturar mi equipaje
Ke-eh'-roh fac-too-rar' mee eh-ke-pah'-heh

Here are the luggage tickets (checks)
Aquí están los talones
Ah-kee' es-tahn' lohs tah-lau'-nes

Put these bags in the train
Ponga estas maletas en el tren
Paun'-gah es'-tas mah-leh'-tas en el trehn

Here are my bags
Estas son mis maletas
Es'-tas saun mees mah-leh'-tas

At what time does the train for... leave?
¿A qué hora sale el tren para...?
Ah keh' au'-rah sah'-leh el trehn pah'-rah...?

In ten minutes
Dentro de diez minutos
Den'-troh deh de-eth' me-noo'-tohs

The train for... leaves from platform n.º 4
El tren para... sale del andén n.º 4
El tren pah'-rah... sah'-leh del ahn-den' noo'-meh-rau 4

Is this the train for...?
¿Es éste el tren para...?
Es es'-teh el trehn pah'-rah...?

Where is the newspaper shop?
¿Dónde está el quiosco de periódicos?
Daun'-deh es-tah' el ke-aus'-koh deh peh-re-au'-de-cohs?

A railway timetable
Un horario, por favor
Oon au-rah'-re-oh, paur fah-vaur'

All aboard!
Sres. viajeros, al tren
Seh-nyau'-res ve-ah-heh'-rohs, ahl tren

This seat is taken
Este asiento está ocupado
Es'-teh ah-se-en'-toh es-tah'au-coo-pah'-doh

Why is the train stopping?
¿Por qué se para el tren?
Paur keh' seh pah'-rah el tren?

We stop here half an hour
Paramos aquí media hora
Pah-rah'-mohs ah-kee' meh'-de-ah au'-rah

May I smoke, madam?
¿Me permite fumar, señora?
Meh pehr-mee'-the foo-mar', seh-nyau'-rah?

Please, close the window
Por favor, cierre la ventanilla
Paur fah-vaur', the-er'-reh lah ven-tah nee'-lya

Tickets, please
Billetes, por favor
Be-lyeh'-tes, paur fah-vaur'

Where is the dining-car?
¿Dónde está el coche restaurante?
Daun'-de es-tah' el cau'-cheh res-tah-oo-rahn'-teh?

Must I change trains?
¿Hay trasbordo en el trayecto?
Ah'-ee tras-baur'-doh en el trah-yec'-toh?

You must change trains at...
Debe cambiar de tren en...
Deh'-beh cahm-be-ar' de tren en...

Prepare my berth
Prepare mi cama
Preh-pah'-reh mee cah'-mah

Call me at seven
Avíseme a las siete
Ah-vee'-seh-meh ah las se-eh'-teh

How many stations are there to...?
¿Cuántas estaciones faltan para llegar a...?
Coo-ahn'-tas es-ta-the-au'-nes fahl'-tahn pah'-rah lyeh-gar' ah...?

At what time do we arrive?
¿A qué hora llegamos?
Ah keh' au'-rah lyeh-gah'-mohs?

We are fifteen minutes late
Llevamos 15 minutos de retraso
Lyeh-vah'-mohs keen'-theh mee-noo'-tohs de reh-trah'-soh

Take my bags
Recoja mi equipaje
Reh-cau'-hah mee eh-ke-pah'-he

This handbag is not mine
Este maletín no es mío
Es'-teh mah-leh-teen' no es mee'-oh

Find me a taxi
Búsqueme un taxi
Boos'-keh-meh oon tak'-se

THE CAR
Service and breakdowns

Oil
Aceite
Ah-thei'-teh

Accelerator
Acelerador
Ah-theh-leh-rah-daur'

Water
Agua
Ah'-goo-ah

Air
Aire
Ah'-e-reh

Breakdown
Avería
Ah-veh-ree'-ah

Battery
Batería
Bah-teh-ree'-ah

Connecting rod
Biela
Be-eh'-lah

Coil
Bobina
Bau-bee'-nah

Pump
Bomba
Baum'-bah

Plug
Bujía
Boo-hee'-ah

Gear box
Caja de cambios
Cah'-hah deh cahm'-be-ohs

Chamber
Cámara
Cah' mah rah

Bonnet	**Carburetor**	**Crankcase**
Capó	Carburador	Cárter
Cah-pauh'	*Car-boo-rah-daur'*	*Car'-ter*
Crankshaft	**Safety belt**	**Fan belt**
Cigüeñal	Cinturón de seguridad	Correa de ventilador
The-goo-eh-nyahl'	*Thin-too-raun' deh seh-goo-re-dahd'*	*Caur-reh'-ah deh ven-te-lah-daur'*
Cylinder head	**Tank**	**De-clutch**
Culata	Depósito	Desembrague
Coo-lah'-tah	*Deh-pau'-se-toh*	*Des-em-brah'-gheh*
Dynamo	**Clutch**	**Head-light (fog light)**
Dinamo	Embrague	Faro (antiniebla)
De-nah'-moh	*Em-brah'-gheh*	*Fah'-roh (ahn-te-ne-eh'-blah)*
Filter	**Brake**	**Fuse**
Filtro	Freno	Fusible
Feel'-troh	*Freh'-noh*	*Foo-see'-bleh*
Petrol (gasoline)	**Jack**	**Wing (fender)**
Gasolina	Gato	Guardabarros
Gah-sau-lee'-nah	*Gah'-toh*	*Goo-ar-dah-bar'-rohs*
Blinking-light	**Cylinder head joint**	**Screen wiper**
Intermitente	Junta de culata	Limpia-para-brisas
In-ter-me-ten'-teh	*Hoon'-tah deh coo-lah'-tah*	*Leem-pe-ah-pah-rah-bree'-sas*

Ignition key	**Registration number**	**Mixture**
Llave de contacto	Matrícula	Mezcla
Lyah'-veh deh caun-tac'-toh	*Mah-tree'-coo-lah*	*Meth'-clah*
Engine	**Tyre (tire)**	**Lever**
Motor	Neumático	Palanca
Mau-taur'	*Neh-oo-mah'-te-coh*	*Pah-lahn'-cah*
Windscreen	**Bumper**	**Pedal**
Parabrisas	Parachoques	Pedal
Pah-rah-bree'-sas	*Pah-rah-chau'-kes*	*Peh-dahl'*
Lights	**Puncture**	**Piston**
Pilotos	Pinchazo	Pistón
Pe-lau'-tohs	*Peen-chah'-thoh*	*Pees-taun'*
Contact braker points	**Door**	**Radiator**
Platinos	Portezuela	Radiador
Plah-tee'-nohs	*Paur-teh-thoo-eh'-lah*	*Rah-de-ah-daur'*
Wheel	**Piston rings**	**Exhaust pipe**
Rueda	Segmentos	Tubo de escape
Roo-eh'-dah	*Seg-men'-tohs*	*Too'-boh deh es-cah'-peh*
Valve	**Steering wheel**	
Válvula	Volante	
Vahl'-voo-lah	*Vau-lahn'-teh*	

I have a flat tyre
Tengo un neumático deshinchado
Ten'-goh oon neh-oo-mah'-te-coh des-een-chah'-doh

Check the plugs
Repase las bujías
Reh-pah'-se las boo-hee'-as

Charge the battery
Cargue la batería
Car'-gheh lah bah-teh-ree'-ah

I have a breakdown
Tengo avería
Ten'-goh ah-veh-ree'-ah

My car has broken down ... kilometers from here
Mi coche se ha averiado a ... kilómetros de aquí
Mee cau'-cheh seh ah ah-veh-re-ah'-doh ah ... ke-lau'-meh-trohs deh ah-kee'

Can you tow my car?
¿Puede usted remolcarme?
Poo-eh'-deh oos-ted' reh-maul-car'-meh?

The car won't start
El coche no arranca
El cau'cheh no ar-rahn'-cah

The radiator leaks
El radiador pierde
El rah-de-ah-daur' pe-er'-deh

The motor has seized
El motor está agarrotado
El mau-taur' es-tah' ah-gar-rau-tah'-doh

The clutch does not work
El embrague no funciona
El em-brah'-gheh no foon-the-au'-nah

Where is the garage?
¿Dónde está el garaje?
Daun'-deh es-tah' el gah-rah'-heh?

49

Is it open at night?
¿Está abierto por la noche?
Es-tah' ah-be-er'-toh paur la nau'-cheh?

Fill her up
Llene el depósito
Lheh'-neh el deh-pau'-se-toh

Put in twenty liters, please
Veinte litros, por favor
Veh'-in-teh lee'-trohs, paur fah-vaur'

It is ... pesetas
Son ... pesetas
Saun ... peh-seh'-tas

I need some oil (water)
Necesito aceite (agua)
Neh-the-see'-toh ah-thei'-teh (ah'-goo-ah)

I want the oil changed
Quiero cambiar el aceite
Ke-eh'-roh cahm-be-ar' el ah-thei'-teh

Can you have my car greased?
¿Pueden engrasar el coche?
Poo-eh'-den en-grah-sar' el cau'-cheh?

Fill up the radiator
Llene el radiador
Lyeh'-neh el rah-de-ah-daur'

Examine the tyres
Revise los neumáticos
Reh-vee'-seh lohs neh-oo-mah'-te-cohs

Have you spares?
¿Tiene usted repuestos?
Te-eh'-neh oos-ted' reh-poo-es'-tohs?

We have to send for spare parts
Tenemos que pedir recambios
Teh-neh'-mohs keh peh-deer' reh-cahm'-be-ohs

Is there a mechanic?
¿Tienen mecánico?
Te-eh'-nen meh-cah'-ne-coh?

How long will it take to wash it (to repair it)?
¿Cuánto tiempo tardarán en lavarlo (repararlo)?
Coo-ahn'-toh te-em'-poh tahr-dah-rahn' en lah-var'-loh (reh-pah-rar'-loh)?

It will take three days
Tardará tres días
Tar-dah-rah' tres dee'-as

It needs new plugs
Necesita bujías nuevas
Neh-theh-see'-tah boo-hee'-as noo-eh'-vas

Can you repair it temporarily?
¿Pueden hacer un arreglo provisional?
Poo-eh'-den ah-thehr' oon ahr-reh'-gloh prau-ve-se-au-nahl'?

The carburetor needs repairing
Hay que reparar el carburador
Ah'-ee keh reh-pah-rar' el car-boo-rah-daur'

What is the matter?
¿Qué le pasa?
Keh' leh pah'-sah?

The battery is dead
La batería está descargada
Lah bah-teh-ree'-ah es-tah' des-car-gah'-dah

Where is the police station (hospital)?
¿Dónde está la comisaría (el hospital)?
Daun'-deh es-tah' lah cau-me-sah-ree'-ah (el aus-pe-tahl')?

51

There has been an accident ... kilometers from here
Hay un accidente a ... kilómetros de aquí
Ah'-ee oon ac-thee-den'-teh ah ... ke-lau'-meh-trohs deh ah-kee'

There is someone injured
Hay heridos
Ah'-ee eh-ree'-dohs

Call a doctor
Llamen a un médico
Lyah'-men ah oon meh'-de-coh

Are you hurt?
¿Está usted herido?
Es-tah' oos-ted' eh-ree'-doh?

Here is my insurance cover
Aquí está mi póliza de seguros
Ah-kee'es-tah' mee pau'-le-thah deh seh-gooh'-rohs

THE CAR

Rent-a-car		Car on road

North
Norte
Naur'-teh

South
Sur
Soor

East
Este
Es'-teh

West
Oeste
Au-es'-teh

This way
Por aquí
Paur ah-kee'

That way
Por allá
Paur ah-lyah'

To the right (left)
A la derecha (izquierda)
Ah lah deh-reh'-chah (eeth-ke-er'-dah)

Far
Lejos
Leh'-hohs

Near
Cerca
Ther'-cah

I want to hire a car
Deseo alquilar un coche
Deh-seh'-oh ahl-ke-lar' oon cau'-cheh

Here is my driving licence
Aquí está mi carnet de conducir
Ah-kee' es-tah' mee car-net' deh caun-doo-theer'

53

What is the cost per km (per day)?
¿Cuál es el precio por km (por día)?
Coo-ahl' es el preh'-the-oh paur ke-loh'-meh-troh (paur dee'-ah)?

Insurance included
Incluido el seguro
In-cloo-ee'-doh el seh-goo'-roh

Must I leave a deposit?
¿Debo dejar fianza?
Deh'-boh deh-har' fe-ahn'-thah?

Can I park here?
¿Puedo dejar mi coche aquí?
Poo-eh'-doh deh-har' mee cau'-cheh ah-kee'?

How long?
¿Cuánto tiempo?
Coo-ahn'-toh te-em'-poh?

All night long
Toda la noche
Tau'-dah lah nau'-cheh

How far is ...?
¿A qué distancia está ...?
Ah keh' dis-tahn'-the-ah es-tah'?

There are some ... kilometers
Son unos ... kilómetros
Saun oo'-nohs ... ke-lau'-meh-trohs

It is not far
No está lejos
Nau es-tah' leh'-hohs

The road to ..., please
Para ir a ..., por favor
Pah'rah eer ah ..., paur fa-vaur'

This way
En esta dirección
En es'-tah de-rec-the-aun'

Follow on, you are going the right way
Siga, va en dirección correcta
Se'-gah, vah en de-rec-the-aun' caur-rec'-tah

Is the road good?
¿Es buena la carretera?
Es boo-eh'-nah lah car-reh-teh'-rah?

Yes, but there are many bends
Sí, pero con muchas curvas
See, peh'-roh caun moo'-chas coor'-vas

Is this the way to ...?
¿Es esta la carretera para ...?
Es es'-tah lah car-reh-teh'-rah pah'-rah ...?

Turn left at the next crossroads
Gire a la izquierda en el primer cruce
Hee'-reh ah lah eeth-ke-er'-dah en el pre-mer' croo'-theh

Can you draw me a map?
¿Puede hacerme un croquis?
Poo-eh'-deh ah-ther'-meh oon crau'-kis?

Can you recommend me a good restaurant?
¿Puede recomendarme un buen restaurante?
Poo-eh'-deh reh-cau-men-dar'-meh oon boo-en' res-tah-oo-rahn'-teh?

Go to ... You will be satisfied
Vaya a ... Le atenderán bien
Vah'-yah ah ... Leh ah-ten-deh-rahn' be-en'

Is it far?
¿Está lejos?
Es-tah' leh'-hohs?

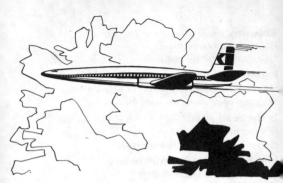

THE PLANE

Airport
Aeropuerto

Ah-eh-rau-poo-er'-toh

Runway
Pista de aterrizaje

Pees'-tah deh ah-ter-re-thah'-heh

Propeller
Hélice

Eh'-le-theh

Pilot
Piloto

Pe-lau'-toh

Radio officer
Radio-telegrafista

Rah-de-au-teh-leh-grah-fees'-tah

Air hostess
Azafata

Ah-thah-fah'-tah

Safety belt
Cinturón de seguridad

Thin-too-raun' deh seh-goo-re-dahd'

Flight
Vuelo

Voo-eh'-loh

Engine
Motor

Mau-taur'

Seat
Butaca

Boo-tah'-cah

Terminus
Estación terminal

Es-tah-the-aun' ter-me-nahl'

I want a reservation for the first flight to ...
Deseo una reserva para el próximo vuelo a ...
Deh-seh'-oh oo'-nah reh-ser'-vah pah'-rah el prauc'-se-moh voo-eh'-loh ah ...

How much free luggage is allowed?
¿Cuánto equipaje admiten libre de pago?
Coo-ahn'-toh eh-ke-pah'-heh ad-mee'-ten lee'-breh deh pah'-goh?

How can I get to the airport?
¿Cómo puedo trasladarme al aeropuerto?
Cau'-moh poo-eh'-doh trahs-lah-dar'-meh ahl ah-eh-rau-poo-er'-toh?

In the airport bus
En el autocar de la compañía
En el ah-oo-tau-car' deh luh caum-pah nyee'-ah

The loudspeaker will warn you
El altavoz le avisará
El ahl-tah-vauth' leh ah-ve-sah-rah'

Passengers for flight ... go to door ...
Se ruega a los pasajeros del vuelo ... pasen a la puerta ...
Seh roo-eh'-gah ah lohs pah-sah-heh'-rohs del voo-eh'-loh ... pah'-sen ah lah poo-er'-tah ...

No smoking
Prohibido fumar
Prau-e-bee'-doh foo-mar'

Fasten your seat belts, please
Por favor, abróchense los cinturones
Paur fah-vaur', ah-brau'-chen-seh lohs thin-too-rau'-nes

You must not smoke until we are in full flight
No deben fumar hasta que estemos en pleno vuelo
No deh'-ben foo-mar' as'-tah keh es-teh'-mohs en pleh'-noh voo-eh'-loh

57

Can I have some cotton wool for my ears?
Deme un poco de algodón para los oídos, por favor
Deh'-meh oon pau'-coh deh ahl-gau-daun' pah'-rah lohs oh-ee'-dohs, paur fah-vaur'

Where are we now?
¿Dónde estamos ahora?
Daun'-deh es-tah'-mohs ah-au'-rah?

Do you want to have something?
¿Quiere tomar algo?
Ke-eh'-reh tau-mar' ahl'-goh?

One coffee, please
Una taza de café, por favor
Oo'-nah tah'-thah deh cah-feh', paur fah-vaur'

There is some fog
Hay algo de niebla
Ah'-ee ahl'-goh deh ne-eh'-blah

We shall land in ten minutes
Aterrizaremos dentro de diez minutos
Ah-ter-re-thah-reh'-mohs den'-troh deh de-eth' me-noo'-tohs

The plane is going down
El avión está descendiendo
El ah-ve-aun' es-tah' des-then-de-en'-doh

Pick up your luggage at the terminus
Retire su equipaje en la estación terminal
Reh-tee'-reh soo eh-ke-pah'-heh en lah es-tah-the-aun' tehr-me-nahl'

It has been a very pleasant trip
Ha sido un viaje muy agradable
Ah se'-doh oon ve-ah'-heh moo'-e ah-grah-dah'-bleh

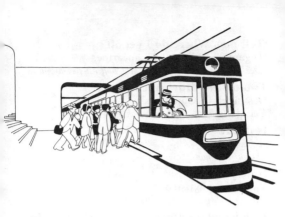

BUSES AND UNDERGROUND (SUBWAY)

I want to go to ...
Quiero ir a ...
Ke-eh'-roh eer ah ...

What bus must I take?
¿Qué autobús debo tomar?
Keh'ah-oo-tau-boos' deh'-boh tau-mar'?

Stop here
Pare aquí
Pah'-reh ah-kee'

Does this bus pass by ...?
¿Pasa este autobús por ...?
Pah'-sah es'-teh ah-oo-tau-boos' paur ...?

The underground (subway) leaves you very near
El metro le deja muy cerca
El meh'-troh leh deh'-hah moo'-e ther'-cah

(Tell me). Where do I get off?
(Dígame). ¿Dónde debo apearme?
(Dee'-gah-meh). Daun'-deh deh'-boh ah-peh-ar'-meh?

Two tickets. How much?
Dos billetes. ¿Cuánto es?
Daus be-lyeh'-tes. Coo'-ahn-toh es?

Is it far?
¿Está lejos?
Es-tah' leh'-hohs?

Here you are
Ya ha llegado usted
Yah ah lyeh-gah'-doh oos-ted'

Is this seat occupied?
¿Está ocupado este asiento?
Es-tah' au-coo-pah'doh es'teh ah-se-en'-toh?

From what time to what time does the bus pass by?
¿Cada cuánto tiempo pasa el autobús?
Cah'dah coo-an'-toh te-em'-poh pah'-sah el ah-oo-tau-boos?

TAXIS

Take me to ... street
Lléveme a la calle ...
Lyeh'-veh-meh ah lah cah'-lyeh ...

Drive around the city
Deme una vuelta por la ciudad
Deh'-meh oo'-nah voo-el'-tah paur lah the-oo-dahd'

How much is the fare for ...?
¿Cuánto me costaría ir a ...?
Coo-ahn'-toh meh caus-tah-ree'-ah eer ah ...?

60

Wait a minute
Espéreme un momento
Es-peh'-reh-meh oon moh-men'-toh

I shall return at once
Vuelvo ahora mismo
Voo-el'-voh ah-au'-rah mees'-moh

I cannot wait
No puedo esperar
No poo-eh'-doh-es-peh-rar'

I shall wait for you on the opposite side
Le espero enfrente
Leh es-peh'-roh en-fren'-teh

Here you are
Ya hemos llegado
Yah eh'-mohs lyeh-gah'-doh

How much is it?
¿Qué le debo?
Keh' leh deh'-boh?

That is for you
Tenga, para usted
Ten'-gah, pah'-rah oos-ted'

Come tomorrow at 10 o'clock
Venga a buscarme mañana a las diez
Ven'-gah ah boos-car'-meh mah-nyah'-nah ah lahs de-eth'

Take me to a good hotel
Lléveme a un buen hotel
Lyeh'-veh-meh ah oon boo-en' au-tel'

Is it very far?
¿Está muy lejos?
Es-tah' moo'-e leh'-hohs?

Do you know where is ...?
¿Sabe usted dónde está ...?
Sah'-beh oos-ted' daun'-deh es-tah' ...?

HOTEL

In every good hotel you will have an adequate service by interpreters, but you cannot hope to have one of them at your exclusive disposal. With the YALE GUIDE you will be sure of making yourself understood at any moment and you will be able to benefit to the utmost from your stay and from the delicious Spanish food.

ARRIVING

Manager	**Porter (janitor)**	**Valet**
Gerente	Portero	Botones
Heh-ren'-teh	*Paur-teh'-roh*	*Bau-tau'-nes*
Head waiter	**Waiter**	**Chamber maid**
Maitre	Camarero	Camarera
Metr	*Cah-mah-reh'-roh*	*Cah-mah-reh'-rah*
Dining-room	**Room**	**Bar**
Comedor	Dormitorio	Bar
Cau-meh-daur'	*Daur-me-tau'-re-oh*	*Bar*

Bath room	**Bed**	**Key**
Cuarto de baño	Cama	Llave
Coo-ar'-toh deh	*Cah'-mah*	*Lyah'-veh*
bah'-nyoh		

Please, have you any room free?
Por favor, ¿tienen habitaciones libres?
Paur fah-vaur', te-eh'-nen ah-be-tah-the-au'-nes lee'-bres?

I have booked a room
Tengo reservada una habitación
Ten'-goh reh-ser-vah'-dah oo'-na ah-be-tah-the-aun'

I want an outside (inside) room
Desearía una habitación exterior (interior)
Deh-seh-ah-ree'-ah oo'-nah ah-be-tah-the-aun' ex-teh-re-aur' (in-teh-re-aur')

For one person
Para una persona
Pah'-rah oo'-nah per-sau'-nah

For two persons
Para dos personas
Pah'-rah daus per-sau'-nas

I want a room with a bath
Quiero una habitación con baño
Ke-eh'-roh oo'-nah ah-be-tah-the-aun' caun bah'-nyoh

How long will you be staying, sir?
¿Cuánto tiempo piensa quedarse, señor?
Coo-ahn'-toh te-em'-poh pe-en'-sah keh-dar'-seh, seh-nyaur'?

One night
Esta noche
Es-tah nau'-cheh

Some three days
Unos tres días
Oo'-nohs tres dee'-as

How much is it?
¿Cuál es el precio?
Coo-ahl' es el preh'-the-oh?

Do you want just the room, half board or full board?
¿Desea la habitación sola, media pensión o pensión completa?
Deh-seh'-ah lah ah-be-tah-the-aun' sau'-lah, meh'-de-ah pen-se-aun' au pen-se-aun' caum-pleh'-tah?

Breakfast included?
¿Incluido el desayuno?
In-cloo-ee'-doh el deh-sah-yoo'-noh?

May I see the room?
¿Podría ver la habitación?
Pau-dree'-ah ver lah ah-be-tah-the-aun'?

It is too dark
Es demasiado oscura
Es deh-mah-se-ah'-doh aus-coo'-rah

It is too noisy
Hay demasiado ruido
Ah'-ee deh-mah-se-ah'-doh roo-ee'-doh

Do you like this one?
¿Le gusta ésta?
Leh goos'-tah es'-tah?

All right, thank you
Está bien, gracias
Es-tah' be-en', grah'-the-as

Send up my luggage, please
Suban mi equipaje, por favor
Soo'-bahn mee eh-ke-pah'-heh, paur fah-vaur'

THE STAY

Water	**Soap**	**Towel**
Agua	Jabón	Toalla
Ah'-goo-ah	*Hah-baun'*	*Tau-ah'-lyah*

Telephone directory	**Clothing**	**Blanket**
Guía telefónica	Ropa	Manta
Ghee'-ah teh-leh-fau'-ne-cah	*Rau'-pah*	*Mahn'-tah*

Writing paper	**Envelope**	**Stamp**
Papel de cartas	Sobre	Sello
Pah-pel' deh cahr'-tas	*Sau'-breh*	*Seh'-lyoh*

Window	**Door**	**Glass**
Ventana	Puerta	Vaso
Ven-tah'-nah	*Poo-er'-tah*	*Vah'-soh*

My key, please, number ...
Mi llave, por favor, número ...
Me lyah'-veh, paur fa-vaur', noo'-meh-roh ...

Are there any letters for me?
¿Hay alguna carta para mí?
Ha'-e ahl-goo'-nah car'-tah pah'-rah mee?

Send the valet
Envíeme un botones
En-vee'-eh-meh oon bau-tau'-nes

Come in!
¡Adelante!
Ah-deh-lahn'-teh!

Where is the telephone directory?
¿Dónde está la guía telefónica?
Daun'-deh es-tah' lah ghee'-ah teh-leh-fau'-ne-cah?

65

The water is cold
El agua está fría
El ah'-goo-ah es-tah' free'-ah

Bring towels, soap
Tráigame toallas, jabón
Trah'-e-gah-meh tau-ah'-lyahs, hah-baun'

Send my clothes to the laundry
Encárguese de que me laven la ropa
En-car'-gheh-seh deh keh meh lah'-ven lah rau'-pah

Please, polish (shine) my shoes
¿Podrían limpiarme los zapatos?
Pau-dree'-ahn leem'-pe-ar'-meh lohs thah-pah'-tohs?

Please, sew this button, iron (press) my trousers?
¿Podrían coserme este botón? ¿planchar mi pantalón?
Pau-dreeh'-ahn cau-ser'-meh es'-teh bau-taun'?, plahn-char' me pahn-tah-laun'?

This is for the laundry
Esto es para lavar
Es'-toh es pah'-rah lah-var'

It will be ready tomorrow
Estará listo para mañana
Es-tah-rah' lees'-toh pah'-rah mah-nyah'-nah

Please, send for a taxi
Búsqueme un taxi, por favor
Boos'-keh-meh oon tak'-see, paur fah-vaur'

Have you a street plan?
¿Tiene usted un plano de la ciudad?
Te-eh'-neh oos-ted' oon plah'-noh deh lah the-oo-dahd'?

I am cold. Please, put another blanket on the bed
Tengo frío. Ponga otra manta en la cama, por favor
Ten'-goh free'-oh. Paun'-gah au'-trah mahn'-tah en la cah'-mah, paur fah-vaur'

Please call me tomorrow at eight o'clock
Sírvase llamarme mañana temprano, a las ocho
Seer'-vah-seh lyah-mar'-meh mah-nyah'-nah tem-prah'-noh, ah las au'-choh

THE DEPARTURE

I shall leave tomorrow morning at ...
Marcharé mañana por la mañana a ...
Mahr-chah-reh' mah-nyah'-nah paur lah mah-nyah'-nah ah ...

Prepare my bill, please
Prepare mi cuenta, por favor
Preh-pah'-reh mee coo-en'-tah, paur fa-vaur'

Please check it. I have been here only two nights, not three
¿Quiere repasarla? Sólo he estado dos noches, no tres
Ke-eh'-reh reh-pah-sar'-lah? Sau'-loh eh es-tah'-doh daus nau'-ches, no tres

Thank you. Is everything included?
Gracias. ¿Está todo incluido?
Grah'-the-as. Es-tah' tau'-doh in-cloo-ee'-doh?

Send down my luggage, please
Sírvase bajar mis maletas
Seer'-vah-seh bah-har' mees mah-leh'-tas

MEALS

Breakfast	Dinner	Supper
Desayuno	Comida	Cena
Des-ah-yoo'-noh	*Cau-mee'-dah*	*The'-nah*

Diet	Menu
Régimen	Carta
Reh'-he-men	*Car'-tah*

At what time is dinner (supper) served?
¿A qué hora se sirve la comida (la cena)?
Ah keh' au'-rah seh seer'-veh lah cau-mee'-dah, lah theh'-nah?

Serve my breakfast in my room
Suba el desayuno a mi habitación
Soo'-bah el deh-sah-yoo'-noh ah mee ah-be-tah-thee-aun'

Please do not delay. I am in a hurry
Sírvame en seguida, por favor. Tengo prisa
Seer'-vah-meh en seh-ghee'dah, paur fah-vaur'. Ten'-goh pree'-sah

I shall have today's menu
Tomaré el menú del día
Tau-mah-reh' el meh-noo' del dee'-ah

Bring me a diet meal, please
Tráigame por favor una comida de régimen
Trah'-e-gah-meh paur fa-vaur' oo'-nah cau-mee'-dah deh reh'-he-men

I shall not be in for dinner. May I have something to take out?
No vendré a comer. ¿Puede prepararme una bolsa de comida?
No ven-dreh' ah cau-mer'. Poo-eh'-deh preh-pah-rar'-meh oo'-nah baul'-sah deh cau-mee'-dah?

May I have something at this time?
¿Podría tomar algo a esta hora?
Pau-dree'-ah tau-mar' ahl'-goh ah es'-tah au'-rah?

Dining room is closed
El comedor está cerrado
El cau-meh-daur' es-tah' cer-rah'-doh

Charge it on my bill. Room number ...
Póngalo en mi cuenta. Habitación número ...
Paun'-gah-loh en mee coo-en'-tah. Ah-be-ta-thee-aun' noo'-meh-roh ...

IN THE RESTAURANT

Although you will find a menu with a price list in all restaurants, it will always be necessary to talk a little with the waiter, asking him to explain what some dishes consist of or how to choose the suitable drink.

Possessing the YALE GUIDE will be invaluable. Take a glimpse at these phrases when you have the chance.

THE RESTAURANT

Table cloth	Napkin	Glass
Mantel	Servilleta	Vaso (copa)
Mahn-tel'	*Ser-vee-lyeh'-tah*	*Vah'-soh (cau'-pah)*

Cup	Menu	Bill (check)
Taza	Menú	Cuenta
Tah'-thah	*Meh-noo'*	*Coo-en'-tah*

Fork
Tenedor
Teh-neh-daur'

Spoon
Cuchara
Coo-chah'-rah

Knife
Cuchillo
Coo-chee'-lyoh

Glass
Vaso
Vah'-soh

Dish
Plato
Plah'-toh

Bread
Pan
Pahn

Wine
Vino
'ee'-noh

Soup
Sopa
Sau'-pa

Shellfish
Marisco
Mah-rees'-coh

Fish
Pescado
'es-cah'-doh

Meat
Carne
Cahr'-neh

Fruit
Fruta
Froo'-tah

71

Where can we sit?
¿Dónde podemos sentarnos?
Daun'-deh pau-deh'-mohs sen-tar'-nohs?

Waiter, a table for four
Camarero, una mesa para cuatro
Cah-mah-reh'-roh, oo-nah meh'-sah pah'-rah coo-ah'-troh

The menu, please
Deme la carta
Deh'-meh lah car'-tah

What is your speciality?
¿Cuál es la especialidad de la casa?
Coo-ahl' es lah es-pe-thee-ah-le-dahd' deh lah cah'-sah?

Which wine do you recommend?
¿Qué vino me recomienda?
Keh' vee'-noh meh reh-cau-me-en'-da?

I am on a diet
Estoy a régimen
Es-tau'-e ah reh'-he-men

Bring us ...
Tráiganos ...
Trah'-e-gah-nohs ...

First of all, I want a chicken soup
Quisiera comenzar con un consomé
Ke-se-eh'-rah cau-men-thar' caun oon caun-sau-meh'

Afterwards I shall have a rare steak
Después tomaré un bistec poco hecho
Des-poo-es' tau-mah-reh' oon bee-stec' pau'-coh eh'-choh

Enough, thanks
Bastante, gracias
Bas-tahn'-teh, grah'-thee-as

More, please
Sírvame más, por favor
Seer'-vah-meh mas, paur fa-vaur'

No sauce
Sin salsa
Seen sahl'-sah

Bring us some mineral water
Tráiganos agua mineral
Trah'-e-gah-nohs ah'-goo-ah me-neh-rahl'

The bill (check), please
La cuenta, por favor
Lah coo-en'-tah, paur fah-vaur'

Is the tip included?
¿Está incluido el servicio (propina)?
Es-tah' in-cloo-ee'-doh el ser-vee'-thee-oh (prau-pee'-nah)?

KITCHEN TERMS

Boiled	**Light fried**	**Fried**
Cocido	Sofrito	Frito
Cau-thee'-doh	*Sau-free'-toh*	*Free'-toh*
Braised	**Roasted**	**Grilled**
Braseado	Asado	A la parrilla
Brah-seh-ah'-doh	*Ah-sah'-doh*	*Ah lah par-ree'-lyah*
Raw	**Very rare**	**Rare, underdone**
Crudo	Muy poco hecho	Poco hecho
Croo'-doh	*Moo'-e pau'-coh eh'-choh*	*Pau'-coh eh'-choh*

Medium	**Well done**	**Baked**
Regular	Bien hecho	Al horno
Reh-goo-lar'	*Be-en' eh'-choh*	*Ahl aur'-noh*

Baked
Guisado
Ghee-sah'-doh

CONDIMENTS AND DISHES
Condiments

Oil	**Vinegar**	**Mustard**
Aceite	Vinagre	Mostaza
Ah-thei'-teh	*Vee-nah'-greh*	*Maus-tah'-thah*

Salt	**Black pepper**	**Red pepper**
Sal	Pimienta negra	Pimienta roja
Sahl	*Pe-me-en'-tah*	*Pe-me-en'-tah*
	neh'-grah	*rau'-hah*

Soups and «pasta»

Broth	**Canaloni**	**Consommé**
Caldo	Canalones	Consomé
Cahl'-doh	*Cah-nah-lau'-nes*	*Caun-sau-meh'*

Vermicelli	**Macaroni**	**Purée**
Fideos	Macarrones	Puré
Fe-deh'-ohs	*Mah-cahr-rau'-nes*	*Poo-reh'*

Ravioli	**Soup**	**Tallarini**
Ravioli	Sopa	Tallarines
Rah-ve-au'-le	*Sau'-pah*	*Tah-lyah-ree'-nes*

Eggs

Eggs	**Poached**	**Hard boiled**
Huevos	Escalfados	Duros
Oo-eh'-vohs	*Es-cahl-fah'-dohs*	*Doo'-rohs*

Soft boiled	**Scrambled**	**Omelet**
Pasado por agua	Revueltos	Tortilla
Pah-sah'-doh	*Reh-voo-el'-tohs*	*Taur-tee'-lyah*
paur ah'-goo-ah		

Vegetables

Beans	**Onion**	**Cabbage**
Alubias	Cebolla	Col
Ah-loo'-be-ahs	*Theh-bau'-lyah*	*Caul*

Cauliflower	**Asparagus**	**Spinach**
Coliflor	Espárrago	Espinaca
Cau-le-flaur'	*Es-par'-rah-goh*	*Es-pe-nah'-cah*

Chick-pea	**Lima beans**	**French beans**
Garbanzo	Habas	Judías verdes
		(vainas)
Gahr-bahn'-thoh	*Ah'-bas*	*Hoo-dee'-as ver'-des (vah'-e-nas)*

Lettuce	**Lentils**	**Potato**
Lechuga	Lentejas	Patata
Leh-choo'-gah	*Leh-teh'-hahs*	*Pah-tah'-tah*

Cucumber	**Radishes**	**Mushrooms**
Pepino	Rabanitos	Setas
Peh-pee'-noh	*Rah-bah-nee'-tohs*	*Seh'-tas*

Tomatoes	**Carrots**	**Leek**
Tomates	Zanahorias	Puerro
Tau-mah'-tes	*Thah-nah-au'-re-ahs*	*Poo-ehr'-roh*

Fish and seafood

Clam
Almeja
Ahl-meh'-hah

Eel
Anguila
Ahn-ghee'-lah

Anchovies
Anchoa
Ahn-chau'-ah

Tuna
Atún
Ah-toon'

Cod
Bacalao
Bah-cah-lah'-oh

Crab
Cangrejo
Cahn-greh'-hoh

Squid
Calamar
Cah-lah-mar'

Shrimp
Camarón
Cah-mah-raun'

Lobster
Bogavante
Boh-gah'-bahn-teh

Crayfish
Langosta
Lahn-gaus'-tah

Prawn
Langostino
(gamba)
Lahn-gaus-tee'-noh
(gahm'-bah)

Sole
Lenguado
Len-goo-ah'-doh

Bass
Lubina
Loo-bee'-nah

Mussel
Mejillón
Meh-he-lyaun'

Hake
Merluza
Mer-loo'-thah

Growper
Mero
Meh'-roh

Oyster
Ostra
Aus'-trah

Barnacle
Percebe
Per-theh'-beh

Codling
Pescadilla
Pes-cah-dee'-lyah

Octopus
Pulpo
Pool'-poh

Salmon
Salmón
Sahl-maun'

Trout
Trucha
Troo'-chah

Red mullet
Salmonete
Sahl-mau-neh'-teh

Sardine
Sardina
Sahr-dee'-nah

Smoked salmon
Salmón ahumado
Sahl-maun' ah-oo-mah'-doh

Meats, game and poultry

Roast beef
Asado de vaca
Ah-sah'-doh deh vah'-cah

Woodcock
Becada
Beh-cah'-dah

Steak
Bistec
Be-stec'

Beef
Buey
Boo-ei'

Tripe
Callos
Cah'-lyohs

Pork
Cerdo
Ther'-doh

Quail
Codorniz
Cau-daur-neeth'

Rabbit
Conejo
Cau-neh'-hoh

Mutton
Cordero
Caur-deh'-roh

Cutlet
Chuleta
Choo-leh'-tah

Pheasant
Faisán
Fah-e-sahn'

Hen
Gallina
Gah-lyee'-nah

Liver
Hígado
Ee'-gah-doh

Goose
Ganso
Gahn'-soh

Ham
Jamón
Hah-maun'

Suckling pig
Lechón
Leh-chaun'

Tongue
Lengua
Len'-goo-ah

Hare
Liebre
Le-eh'-breh

Chine of pork
Lomo de cerdo
Lau'-moh deh ther'-doh

Duck
Pato
Pah'-toh

Turkey
Pavo
Pah'-voh

Partridge
Perdiz

Per-deeth'

Pigeon
Pichón

Pe-chaun'

Leg of mutton
Pierna de cordero
Pe-ehr'-nah de caur-deh'-roh

Chicken
Pollo
Pau'-lyoh

Kidneys
Riñones
Re-nyau'-nes

Brains
Sesos
Seh'-sohs

Sirloin
Solomillo
Sau-lau-mee'-lyoh

Veal
Ternera
Ter-neh'-ra

Fruits and desserts

Apricot
Albaricoque
Ahl-bah-re-cau'-keh

Almond
Almendra
Ahl-men'-drah

Hazelnut
Avellana
Ah-veh-lyah'-nah

Cherry
Cereza
Theh-reh'-thah

Plum
Ciruela
Thee-roo-eh'-lah

Dates
Dátiles
Dah'-tee-les

Cream caramel
Flan
Flahn

Strawberry
Fresa
Freh'-sah

Pomegranate
Granada
Grah-nah'-dah

Currant
Grosella
Grau-seh'-lyah

Ice cream
Helado
Eh-lah'-doh

Fig
Higo
Ee'-goh

Tangerine
Mandarina
Mahn'-dah-ree'-nah

Butter
Mantequilla
Mahn-teh-kee'-lyah

Apple
Manzana
Mahn-thah'-nah

Peach
Melocotón
Meh-lau-cau-taun'

Melon
Melón
Meh-laun'

Quince
Membrillo
Mehm-bree'-lyoh

Orange
Naranja
Nah-rahn'-hah

Walnut
Nuez
Noo-eth'

Pie
Pastel
Pahs-tel'

Pear
Pera
Peh'-rah

Pineapple
Piña
Pee'-nyah

Banana
Plátano
Plah'-tah-noh

Cheese	**Cake**	**Apple pie**
Queso	Tarta	Tarta de manzana
Keh'-soh	*Tahr'-tah*	*Tahr'-tah deh mahn-thah'-nah*

Drinks

Mineral water	**Anisette**	**Coffee**
Agua mineral	Anís	Café
Ah'-goo-ah me-neh-rahl'	*Ah-nees'*	*Cah-feh'*

White coffee	**Beer**	**Cocktail**
Café con leche	Cerveza	Coctel
Cah-feh' caun leh'-cheh	*Ther-veh'-thah*	*Cauc'-tel*

Brandy	**Champagne**	**Chocolate**
Coñac	Champán	Chocolate
Cau-nyac'	*Chahm-pahn'*	*Chau-cau-lah'-teh*

Gin	**Milk**	**Lemonade**
Ginebra	Leche	Limonada
He-neh'-brah	*Leh'-cheh*	*Le-mau-nah'-dah*

Sherry	**Rum**	**Cider**
Jerez	Ron	Sidra
Heh-reth'	*Raun*	*See'-drah*

Siphon	**Vermouth**	**White wine**
Sifón	Vermut	Vino blanco
Se-faun'	*Ver-moot'*	*Vee'-noh blahn'-coh*

Red wine	**Orange juice**	
Vino tinto	Zumo de naranja	
Vee'-noh teen'-toh	*Thoo'-moh deh nah-rahn'-hah*	

Lemon juice		**Whisky**
Zumo de limón		Whisky
Thoo'-moh deh le-maun'		*Goo-is'-kee*

79

SHOPPING

Are you sure that you will not be tempted into buying some souvenir or some useful article? But still, it is more likely that you need to buy tobacco or would like to have some photographs developed or have to buy a present. Whatever the case is, the YALE GUIDE will be an enormous help, so that you can find exactly what you want.

COSMETICS

Cleansing cream	Nourishing cream	Beauty milk
Crema limpiadora	Crema nutritiva	Leche de belleza
Creh'-mah leem-pe-ah-dau'-rah	*Creh'-mah noo-tre-tee'-vah*	*Leh'-cheh deh beh-lyeh'-thah*

Cologne water	**Mascara**	**Eyebrow pencil**
Colonia	Rimmel	Lápiz para cejas
Cau-lau'-ne-ah	*Ree'-mel*	*Lah'-peeth pah'-rah theh'-has*
Scented soap	**Lipstick**	**Lip outliner**
Jabón de toca-dor	Lápiz de labios	Perfilador de labios
Hah-baun' deh tau-cah-daur'	*Lah'-peeth deh lah'-be-ohs*	*Per-fe-lah-daur' deh lah'-be-ohs*
Compact makeup	**Makeup cream**	**Makeup powder**
Maquillaje compacto	Maquillaje crema	Maquillaje en polvo
Mah-kee-lyah'-heh caum-pac'-toh	*Mah-kee-lyah'-heh creh'-mah*	*Mah-kee-lyah'-heh en paul'-voh*
Face powder	**Hair removing cream**	**Deodorant**
Polvos faciales	Crema depila-toria	Desodorante
Paul'-vohs fah-thee-ah'-les	*Creh'-mah deh-pe-lah-tau'-re-ah*	*Des-au-dau-rahn'-teh*
Shampoo	**Hair removing tweezers**	**Nail varnish**
Champú	Pinzas depila-torias	Esmalte
Chahm-poo'	*Peen'-thas deh-pe-lah-tau'-re-as*	*Es-mahl'-teh*

Nail varnish remover
Quitaesmalte
Kee-tah-es-mahl'-teh

Can you recommend me a good cleansin cream?

¿Podría aconsejarme una buena crema limpiadora

Pau-dree'-ah ah-caun-seh-har'-meh oo'-nah boo-eh'-nal creh'-mah leem-pe-ah-dau'-rah?

I have very delicate (greasy, dry) skin

Tengo el cutis muy fino (graso, seco)

Ten'-goh el coo'-tis moo'-e fee'-noh (grah'-soh, seh'-coh)

Give me a non oily beauty cream

Deme una crema de belleza que no sea grasienta

Deh'-meh oo'-nah creh'-mah deh beh-lyeh'-thah keh n seh'-ah grah-se-en'-tah

Show me some makeup

Enséñeme algún maquillaje

En-seh'-nyeh-meh ahl-goon' mah-kee-lyah'-heh

Cream or a compact one?

¿En crema o compacto?

En creh'-mah au caum-pac'-toh?

This tone is too dark (clear)

Este tono es demasiado oscuro (claro)

Es'-teh tau'-noh es deh-mah-se-ah'-doh aus-coo'-ro. (clar'-roh)

Give me a smooth hair remover

Deme un depilatorio suave

De'-meh oon deh-pe-lah-tau'-re-oh soo-ah'-veh

Have you a good deodorant?

¿Tiene algún desodorante eficaz?

Te-eh'-neh ahl-goon' des-au-dau-rahn'-teh eh-fe-cath'?

A rose (red) enamel

Un esmalte de uñas rosa (rojo)

Oon es-mahl'-teh deh oo'-nyas rau'-sah (rau'-hoh)

I want something not so loud
Quiero algo más discreto
Ke-eh'-roh ahl'-goh mas dees-creh'-toh

This perfume is too strong. I prefer cologne water
Este perfume es demasiado fuerte. Prefiero agua de colonia
Es'-teh per-foo'-meh es deh-mah-se-ah'-doh foo-er'-teh. Preh-fe-eh'-roh ah'-goo-ah deh cau-lau'-ne-ah

PHARMACY

Sedative	Laxative	Sticking plaster
Calmante	Laxante	Esparadrapo
Cahl-mahn'-teh	*Lac-sahn'-teh*	*Es-pah-rah-drah'-poh*
Alcohol	**Cotton wool**	**Desinfectant**
Alcohol	Algodón en rama	Desinfectante
Ahl-cau-aul'	*Ahl-gau-daun' en rah'-mah*	*Des-in-fec-tahn'-teh*
Tablets	**Cough mixture**	**Pills**
Pastillas	Jarabe	Píldoras
Pas-tee'-lyas	*Hah-rah'-beh*	*Peel'-dau-ras*

83

Cough	Headache	Sunburn
Tos	Dolor de cabeza	Quemaduras de sol
Taus	*Dau-laur' deh cah-beh'-thah*	*Keh-mah-doo'-ras deh saul*

Sanitary towels	Prescription	Thermometer
Paños higiénicos	Receta	Termómetro
Pah'-nyohs e-he-eh'-ne-cohs	*Reh-theh'-tah*	*Tehr-mau'-meh-troh*

Aspirin	Oxygenated water	Toothbrush
Aspirina	Agua oxigenada	Cepillo de dientes
Ahs-pe-ree'-nah	*Ah'-goo-ah auk-se-heh-nah'-dah*	*Theh-pee'-lyoh deh de-en'-tes*

Toothpaste	Shaving brush	Razor blades
Dentífrico	Brocha de afeitar	Hojas de afeitar
Den-tee'-fre-coh	*Brau'-chah deh ah-fei-tar'*	*Au'-has deh ah-fei-tar'*

After shave lotion	Acetone
Loción de afeitado	Acetona
Lau-the-aun' deh ah-fei-tah'-doh	*Ah-theh-tau'-nah*

Give me some cough mixture (tablets)
Deme jarabe (pastillas) para la tos
Deh'-meh hah-rah'-beh (pahs-tee'-lyas) pah'-rah lah taus

Without antibiotics (sulfanilamide). I am allergic
Sin antibióticos (sulfamidas). Soy alérgico
Seen ahn-te-be-au'-te-cohs (sool-fah-mee'-das). Sau'-e ah-ler'-he-coh

Have you anything for sleeplessness? Not barbituricals

¿Tiene algo contra el insomnio? Que no sean barbitúricos

Te-eh'-neh ahl'-goh caun'-trah el in-saum'-ne-oh? Keh nau seh'-ahn bahr-be-too'-re-cohs

Have you any pills for toothache?

¿Tiene píldoras para el dolor de muelas?

Te-eh'-neh peel'-dau-ras pah'-rah el dau-laur' deh moo-eh'-las?

Give me some cream for sunburn

Deme una crema contra las quemaduras del sol

Deh'-meh oo-nah creh'-mah caun'-trah lahs keh-mah-doo'-ras del saul

Give me a good liniment

Deme un buen linimento

Deh'-meh oon boo-en' le-ne-men'-toh

Please, dispatch this prescription

¿Quiere servirme esta receta?

Ke-eh'-reh ser-veer'-meh es'-tah reh-theh'-tah?

I want some pills for seasickness

Quiero unas pastillas contra el mareo

Ke-eh'-roh oo'-nas pas-tee'-lyas caun'-trah el mah-reh'-oh

PHOTOGRAPHY

Camera
Máquina
fotográfica
*Mah'-ke-nah
phau-tau-grah'-
fe-cah*

Lens
Objetivo

Aub-heh-tee'-voh

Trigger
Disparador

Dis-pah-rah-daur'

View-finder
Visor
Ve-saur'

Tripod
Trípode
Tree'-pau-deh

Enlargement
Ampliación
*Ahm-plee-ah-the-
aun'*

Camera film
Película
Peh-lee'-coo-lah

Filter
Filtro
Feel'-troh

Print
Copia
Cau'-pe-ah

Focusing
Enfoque
En-fau'-keh

Size
Tamaño
Tah-mah'-nyoh

Negative
Negativo
Neh-gah-tee'-voh

86

Colour	Black and white	Cover
Color	Blanco y negro	Funda
Cau-laur'	*Blahn'-coh ee neh'-groh*	*Foon'-dah*

Please give me three rolls of film

Haga el favor de darme tres rollos de película

Ah'-gah el fah-vaur' deh dar'-meh tres rau'-lyohs deh peh-lee'-coo-lah

What size, please?

¿De qué tamaño, por favor?

Deh keh' tah-mah'-nyoh, paur fah-vaur'?

Give me a colour film

Deme una película en color

Deh'-meh oo'-nah peh-lee'-coo-lah en cau-laur'

I am sorry, we have just finished them

Lo siento, se nos acaban de terminar

Loh se-en'-toh, seh naus ah-cah'-bahn deh tehr-me-nar'

Please develop this film with two prints of each photograph

Sírvase revelar este rollo y saque dos copias de cada fotografía

Seer'-vah-seh reh-veh-lar' es'-teh rau'-lyoh ee sah'-keh daus cau'-pe-as deh cah'-dah phau-tau-grah-phee'-ah

Can you enlarge these prints?

¿Puede ampliarme estas copias?

Poo-eh'-deh ahm-plee-ar'-meh es'-tas cau'-pe-as?

I want to buy a camera. What make do you recommend?

Quisiera comprar una máquina. ¿Qué marca me aconseja?

Ke-se-eh'-rah caum-prar' oo'-nah mah'-ke-nah. Keh' mar'-cah meh ah-caun-seh'-hah?

SHOPS OR STORES

Night dress
Camisón
Cah-me-saun'

Tie
Corbata
Caur-bah'-tah

Zip
Cremallera
Creh-mah-lyeh'-rah

Corset
Faja
Fah'-hah

Skirt
Falda
Fahl'-dah

Sun glasses
Gafas de sol
Gah'-fas deh saul

Gloves
Guantes
Goo-ahn'-tes

Raincoat
Impermeable
Im-per-meh-ah'-bleh

Pull-over
Jersey
Her-sei'

Garter
Liga
Lee'-gah

Stockings
Medias
(de liga)
*Meh'-de-as
(deh lee-gah)*

Trousers
Pantalón
Pahn-tah-laun'

Handkerchief
Pañuelo
Pah-nyoo-eh'-loh

Tights
Medias (pantys)
*Meh'-de-as
(pahn'-tees)*

Umbrella
Paraguas
Pah-rah'-goo-as

Earrings
Pendientes
Pen-de-en'-tes

Pajamas
Pijama
Pee-hah'-mah

Bracelet
Pulsera
Pool-seh'-rah

Watch
Reloj
Reh-lau'

Hat
Sombrero
Saum-breh'-roh

Ring
Sortija
Saur-tee'-hah

Bra
Sostén
Saus-ten'

Suit
Traje
Trah'-heh

Dress
Vestido
Ves-tee'-doh

Bathing costume
Traje de baño
Trah'-heh deh bah'-nyoh

EN LOS ALMACENES-AT THE SHOPS

Overcoat
Abrigo *Ah-bree'-goh*

Jacket
Americana *Ah-meh-re-cah'-nah*

Beret
Boina *Boi'-nah*

Socks
Calcetines *Cahl-the-tee'-nes*

Underpants
Calzoncillos *Cahl-thaun-thee'lyohs*

Shirt
Camisa *Cah-mee'-sa*

Vest Camiseta
Cah-me-seh'-tah

Belt Cinturón
Theen-too-raun'

Tie Corbata
Caur-bah'-tah

Raincoat
Impermeable
Im-per-meh-ah'-bleh

Jersey
Jersey *Her-sei'*

Trousers Pantalón
Pahn-tah-laun'

89

Cotton	**Leather**	**Lace**
Algodón	Cuero	Encaje
Ahl-gau-daun'	*Coo-eh'-roh*	*En-cah'-heh*
Suede	**Thread**	**Wool**
Gamuza	Hilo	Lana
Gah-moo'-thah	*Ee'-loh*	*Lah'-nah*
Nylon	**Rayon**	**Silk**
Nilón	Rayón	Seda
Ne-laun'	*Rah-yaun'*	*Seh'-dah*
Yellow	**Indigo**	**Blue**
Amarillo	Añil	Azul
Ah-mah-ree'-lyoh	*Ah-nyeel'*	*Ah-thool'*
Beige	**White**	**Grey**
Beige	Blanco	Gris
Beish	*Blahn'-coh*	*Grees*
Mauve	**Brown**	**Purple**
Malva	Marrón	Morado
Mahl'-vah	*Mar-raun'*	*Mau-rah'-doh*
Orange	**Black**	**Red**
Naranja	Negro	Rojo
Nah-rahn'-hah	*Neh'-groh*	*Rau'-hoh*
Rose	**Green**	**Light**
Rosa	Verde	Claro
Rau'-sah	*Ver'-deh*	*Clah'-roh*
Dark	**Dark haired**	**Fair haired**
Oscuro	Moreno	Rubio
Aus-coo'-roh	*Moh-reh'-noh*	*Roo'-be-oh*

Where is the shirt department?
¿Dónde está la sección de camisería?
Daun'-deh es-tah' lah sec-the-aun' deh cah-me-seh-ree'-ah?

On the ground floor
En la planta baja
En lah plahn'-tah bah'-hah

I want two coloured shirts
Quiero dos camisas de color
Ke-eh'-roh daus cah-mee'-sas deh cau-laur'

What size, please?
¿De qué talla, por favor?
De keh' tah'-lyah, paur fah-vaur'?

I prefer poplin
Las prefiero de popelín
Las preh-fe-eh'-roh deh pau-peh-leen'

The skirt is too long (short)
La falda es demasiado larga (corta)
Lah fahl'-dah es deh-mah-se-ah'-doh lar'-gah (caur'-tah)

Try this larger size
Pruébese esta talla mayor
Proo-eh'-beh-seh es'-tah tah'-lyah mah-yaur'

Will they shrink in the wash?
¿Encogen al lavar?
En-cau'-hen ahl lah-var'?

Show me also some ties and handkerchiefs
Enséñeme también corbatas y pañuelos
En-seh'-nyeh-meh tahm-be-en' caur-bah'-tas ee pah-nyoo-eh'-lohs

These are the latest fashion. They are crease proof
Estos son los últimos modelos que hemos recibido. Son inarrugables.
Es'-tohs saun lohs ool'-te-mohs mau-deh'-lohs keh eh'-mohs reh-thee-bee'-doh. Saun in-ar-roo-gah'-bles

I want something not so loud
Las quiero menos chillonas
Las ke-eh'-roh meh'-nohs che-lyau'-nas

How much does this cost?
¿Cuánto vale esto?
Coo-ahn'-toh vah'-leh es'-toh?

It is too expensive
Es demasiado caro
Es deh-mah-se-ah'-doh cah'-roh

Have you something cheaper?
¿Tiene algo más barato?
Te-eh'-neh ahl'-goh mas bah-rah'-toh?

How much does this cloth cost per meter?
¿Cuánto vale el metro de esta tela?
Coo-ahn'-toh vah'-leh el meh'-troh deh es'-tah teh'-lah?

May I try this coat on?
¿Puedo probarme este abrigo?
Poo-eh'-doh prau-bar'-meh es'-teh ah-bree'-goh?

I do not like this colour
No me gusta este color
No meh goos'-tah es'-teh cau-laur'

We have them in every tone
Los tenemos en todos los tonos
Lohs teh-neh'-mohs en tau'-dohs los tau'-nohs

I should like this in rose
Quisiera esto en rosa
Ke-se-eh'-rah es'-toh en rau'-sah

Can you send it to the hotel ...?
¿Pueden enviarme este paquete al hotel ...?
Poo-eh'-den en-ve-ar'-meh es'-teh pah-keh'-teh ahl au-tel' ...?

PRESENTS

Ashtray
Cenicero
Theh-nee-theh'-roh

Cigarette-case
Pitillera
Pe-te-lyeh'-rah

Wallet
Cartera
Car-teh'-rah

Handbag
Bolso
Baul'-soh

Statue
Estatua
Es-tah'-too-ah

Record
Disco
Dees'-coh

Show me some original presents
Quisiera ver algunos regalos originales
Ke-se-eh'-rah ver ahl-goo'-nohs reh-gah'-lohs au-re-he-nah'-les

These handbags are very typical
Estos bolsos son muy típicos
Es-tohs baul'-sohs saun moo'-e tee'-pe-cohs

I like this ashtray in embossed leather
Me gusta este cenicero de cuero repujado
Meh goos'-tah es'-teh theh-nee-theh'-roh deh coo-eh'-roh reh-poo-hah'-doh

Can you initial it?
¿Podrían poner en él unas iniciales?
Pau-dree'-ahn pau-ner' en el oo'-nas e-nee-the-ah'-les?

Have you something with the name of the city?
¿No tiene algún objeto con el nombre de esta ciudad?
No te-eh'-neh ahl-goon' aub-heh'-toh caun el naum'-breh deh es'-tah the-oo-dahd'?

93

How much does this figure cost?
¿Cuánto cuesta esta figurita?
Coo-ahn'-toh coo-es'-tah es'-tah fe-goo-ree'-tah?

I should like to see some typical ceramics
Enséñeme algunos objetos de cerámica típicos
En-seh'-nyeh-meh ahl-goo'-nohs aub-heh'-tohs de theh-rah'-me-cah tee'-pe-cohs

TOYS

Doll	**Meccano**	**Ball**
Muñeca	Mecano	Pelota
Moo-nyeh'-cah	*Meh-cah'-noh*	*Peh-lau'-tah*

Roller-skates	**Rackets**	**Battery**
Patines	Raquetas	Pila
Pah-tee'-nes	*Rah-keh'-tas*	*Pee'-lah*

I want a toy for a boy of ... years
Quiero un juguete para un niño de ... años
Ke-eh'-roh oon hoo-gheh'-teh pah'-rah oon nee'-nyoh deh ... ah'-nyohs

Look at these dolls; they are not too expensive
Vea estas muñecas; no son demasiado caras
Veh'-ah es'-tahs moo-nyeh'-cas; noh saun deh-mah-se-ah'-doh cah'-ras

How much does this electric car cost?
¿Qué vale este coche de pilas?
Keh' vah'-leh es'-teh cau'-cheh deh pee'-las?

I want something cheaper
Quiero algo más barato
Ke-eh'-roh ahl'-goh mas bah-rah'-toh

I think I shall take these roller skates
Creo que llevaré estos patines
Creh'-oh keh lyeh-vah-reh' es'-tohs pah-tee'-nes

Please, show me some educational toy
¿Tiene la bondad de enseñarme algún juego instructivo?
Te-eh'-neh lah baun-dahd' deh en-seh-nyar'-meh ahl-goon' hoo-eh'-goh ins-trooc-tee'-voh?

Is this toy easy to handle?
¿Es fácil de manejar este juguete?
Es fah'-theel deh mah-neh-har' es'-teh hoo-gheh'-teh?

Can you give me two spare batteries?
¿Puede darme dos pilas de repuesto?
Poo-eh'-deh dar'-meh daus pee'-las deh reh-poo-es'-toh?

FOOTWEAR

Shoe	**Slippers**	**Suede**
Zapato	Zapatillas	Ante
Thah-pah'-toh	*Thah-pah-tee'-lyas*	*Ahn'-teh*
Japan	**Sandals**	**Sole**
Charol	Sandalias	Suela
Chah-raul'	*Sahn-dah'-le-as*	*Soo-eh'-lah*
Heel	**Crepe**	**Rubber**
Tacón	Crepé	Goma
Tah-caun'	*Creh-peh'*	*Gau'-mah*

I want a pair of shoes
Deseo un par de zapatos
Deh-seh'-oh oon par deh thah-pah'-tohs

What sort do you want?
¿Cómo los quiere?
Cau'-moh lohs ke-eh'-reh?

Black, white, two-colours
De color negro, blanco, combinados
Deh cau-laur' neh'-groh, blahn'-coh, caum-be-nah'-dohs

With rubber soles, please
Con suela de goma, por favor
Caun soo-eh'-lah deh gauh'-mah, paur fah-vaur'

With high (low, narrow, thick) heels
Con tacón alto (bajo, delgado, grueso)
Caun tah-caun' ahl'-toh (bah'-hoh, del-gah'-doh, groo-eh'-soh)

What size, please?
¿Qué número calza?
Keh' noo'-meh-roh cahl'-thah?

Does this one fit you?
¿Le va bien éste?
Leh vah be-en' es'-teh?

I think they are a little narrow
Creo que me aprietan un poco
Creh'-oh keh meh ah-pre-eh'-tahn oon pau'-coh

Try this size
Pruébese este otro número
Proo-eh'-beh-seh es'-teh au'-troh noo'-meh-roh

This one fits well
Este me está bien
Es'-teh meh es-tah' be-en'

What is their price?
¿De qué precio son?
Deh keh' preh'-the-oh saun?

AT THE TOBACCONIST'S

Tobacconist's
Estanco
Es-tahn'-coh

Tobacco
Tabaco
Tah-bah'-coh

Matches
Cerillas
Theh-ree' lyas

Virginian
Rubio
Roo'-be-oh

Dark
Negro
Neh'-groh

Filter tip
Con filtro
Cauhn' feel'-troh

Cigarette paper
Papel de fumar

Pah-pel' deh foo-mar'

Box of cigars
Caja de puros

Cah'-hah deh poo'-rohs

Packet of cigarettes
Paquete de cigarrillos
Pah-keh'-teh deh thee-gahr-ree'-lyohs

Pipe
Pipa
Pee'-pah

Pouch
Petaca
Peh-tah'-cah

Cigarette-case
Pitillera
Pe-te-lyeh'-rah

Cigarette-holder
Boquilla
Bau-kee'-lyah

Lighter
Mechero
Meh-cheh'-roh

Lighter fuel
Gasolina
Ga-sau-lee'-nah

Give me a packet of filter tipped cigarettes
Deme un paquete de cigarrillos con filtro
Deh'-meh oon pah-keh'-teh deh thee-gah-ree'-lyohs caun feel'-troh

Give me a box of matches also
Deme también una caja de cerillas
Deh'-meh tahm-be-en' oo'-nah cah'-hah deh theh-ree'-lyas

Can you show me some pipes?
¿Puede enseñarme algunas pipas?
Poo-eh'-deh en-seh-nyar'-meh ahl-goo'-nas pee'-pas?

I should like a cigarette-holder
Desearía una boquilla
Deh-seh-ah-ree'-ah oo'-nah bau-kee'-lyah

Show me some postcards
Enséñeme tarjetas postales
En-seh'-nyeh-meh tar-heh'-tas paus-tah'-les

Flints,please
Piedras para el mechero, por favor
Pe-eh'-dras pah'-rah el meh-cheh'-roh, paur fah-vaur'

Can you fill this gas lighter?
¿Puede cargarme este mechero de gas?
Poo-eh'-deh car-gar'-meh es'-teh meh-cheh'-roh deh gas?

AT THE BOOKSELLER'S

Magazine	**Book**	**Newspaper**
Revista	Libro	Periódico
Reh-vees'-tah	*Lee'-broh*	*Peh-re-au'-de-coh*
Writing paper	**Envelope**	**Ink**
Papel de cartas	Sobre	Tinta
Pah-pel' deh car'-tas	*Sau'-breh*	*Teen'-tah*
Ball point pen	**Novel**	**Guide**
Bolígrafo	Novela	Guía
Bau-lee'-grah-foh	*Nau-veh'-lah*	*Ghee'-ah*
Road map	**Street plan**	**Postcard**
Mapa de ca-rreteras	Plano de la ciudad	Tarjeta postal
Mah'-pah deh car-reh-teh'-ras	*Plah'-noh deh lah thee-oo-dahd'*	*Tar-heh'-tah paus-tahl'*

Give me the morning (evening) newspaper
Deme el periódico de la mañana (de la tarde)
*Deh'-meh el peh-re-au'-de-coh deh lah mah-nyah'-nah
(deh lah tahr'-deh)*

Have you any English newspapers?
¿Tienen periódicos ingleses?
Te-eh'-nen pe-re-au'-de-cohs in-gleh'-ses?

Show me some thrillers
Enséñeme algunas novelas policiacas
En-seh'-nyeh-meh ahl-goo'-nas nau-veh'-las pau-le-theeah'-cas

Can you give me a guide and a road map?
¿Puede proporcionarme una guía de la ciudad y
un mapa de carreteras?
*Poo-eh'-deh prau-paur-thee-au-nar'-meh oo'-nah ghee'-a
deh lah thee-oo-dahd' ee oon mah'-pah deh car-reh-teh'-ras?*

Give me a magazine
Deme una revista ilustrada
Deh'-meh oo'-nah re-vees'-tah e-loos-trah'-dah

I should like to see some postcards
Me gustaría ver algunas postales
Meh goos-tah-ree'-ah ver ahl-goo'-nas paus-tah'-les

FLOWERS

White lily
Azucena
Ah-thoo-theh'-nah

Carnation
Clavel
Clah-vel'

Gardenia
Gardenia
Gar-deh'-ne-ah

Jasmin
Jazmín
Hath-meen'

Lily
Lirio
Lee'-re-oh

Mimosa
Mimosa
Me-mau'-sah

Tuberosa
Nardo
Nar'-doh

Orchid
Orquídea
Aur-kee'-deh-ah

Rose
Rosa
Rau'-sah

Tulip
Tulipán
Too-le-pahn'

Violet
Violeta
Ve-au-leh'-tah

Pansy
Pensamiento
Pehn-sah-me-ehn'-toh

I should like to order a bouquet
Desearía encargar un ramo de flores
Deh-seh-ah-ree'-ah en-car-gar' oon rah'-moh deh flau'-res

It is a present and I want it to be nice
Se trata de un regalo y quiero que sea hermoso
Seh trah'-tah deh oon reh-gah'-loh ee ke-eh'-roh keh seh'-ah er-mau'-soh

You can choose roses or carnations in several colours
Puede elegir entre rosas o claveles de varios colores
Poo-eh'-deh eh-leh-heer' en'-treh rau'-sas au clah-veh'-les deh vah'-re-ohs cau-lau'-res

How much does this bouquet of tuberosas cost?
¿Cuánto cuesta este ramo de nardos?
Coo-ahn'-to coo-es'-tah es'-teh rah'-moh deh nar'-dohs?

I shall arrange your bouquet immediately
Prepararé un ramo en seguida
Preh-pah-rah-reh' oon rah'-moh en seh-ghee'-dah

Can you send it tomorrow to this address?
¿Pueden enviarlo mañana a esta dirección?
Poo-eh'-den en-ve-ar'-loh mah-nyah'-nah ah es'-tah derec-the-aun'?

Send this card also, please
Envíe también esta tarjeta, por favor
En-vee'-eh tahm-be-en' es'-tah tar-heh'-tah, paur fah-vaur'

Can I pay in traveller's checks?
¿Puedo pagar con cheques de viaje?
Poo-eh'-doh pah-gar' caun cheh'-kehs deh ve-ah-heh?

ENTERTAINMENTS AND SPORTS

If you are travelling for pleasure, it is obvious that you are going to enjoy yourself. If you are simply travelling on business, there is always one spare hour to add a pleasant variety to your stay abroad. Some of the following phrases can help you to manage in the pictures, in the theatre or in a discotheque.

AMUSEMENTS AND SHOWS
CONCERTS

Music	**Classical**	**Jazz**
Música	Clásico	Jazz
Moo'-se-cah	*Clah'-se-coh*	*Yath*
Opera	**Box (booking) office**	**Cloakroom**
Opera	Taquilla	Guardarropa
Au'-peh-rah	*Tah-kee'-lyah*	*Goo-ar-dar-rau'-pah*

Usher	**Orchestra**
Acomodador	Orquesta
Ah-cau-mau-dah-daur'	*Aur-kes'-tah*

Give me two boxes for this evening's concert
Deme dos palcos para el concierto de esta noche
Deh'-meh daus pahl'-cohs pah'-rah el caun-the-er'-toh deh es'-tah nau'-cheh

I am sorry; I have only stalls on the ground floor
Lo lamento; sólo tengo butacas de platea
Loh lah-men'-toh; sau'-loh ten'-goh boo-tah'-cas deh plah-teh'-ah

A programme, please
Un programa, por favor
Oon prau-grah'-mah, paur fah-vaur'

Can you tell me which opera will be played on Thursday?
¿Podría decirme qué ópera se representará el jueves?
Pau-dree'-ah deh-theer'-meh keh' au'-peh-rah seh reh-preh-sen-tah-rah' el hoo-eh'-ves?

THEATRE

Hall	**Stage**	**Curtain**
Vestíbulo	Escenario	Telón
Ves-tee'-boo-loh	*Es-theh-nah'-re-oh*	*Teh-laun'*

Scenery	**Stall**	**Prompter**
Decorados	Butaca	Apuntador
Deh-cau-rah'-dohs	*Boo-tah'-cah*	*Ah-poon-tah-daur'*

Actor	**Actress**	**Comedy**
Actor	Actriz	Comedia
Ac-taur'	*Ac-treeth'*	*Cau-meh'-de-ah*

Melodrama	**Act**	**Interval**
Melodrama	Acto	Entreacto
Meh-lau-drah'-mah	*Ac'-toh*	*En-treh-ahc'-toh*

Applause	**Whistling**	**Vaudeville**
Aplausos	Silbidos	Vodevil
Ah-plah'-oo-sohs	*Seel-bee'-dohs*	*Vau-deh-veel'*

Two stalls in the centre, please
Dos butacas centrales, por favor
Daus boo-tah'-cas then-trah'-les, paur fah-vaur'

Will row 18 do?
¿Le va bien la fila dieciocho?
Leh vah be-en' lah fee'-lah de-eh-the-au'-choh?

Too far away. I should like something nearer
Demasiado lejos. Prefiero más cerca
Deh-mah-se-ah'-doh le'-hohs. Preh-fe-eh'-roh mas ther'-cah

At what time does the show start?
¿A qué hora comienza la función?
Ah keh' au'-rah cau-me-en'-tha lah foon-the-aun'?

Is it a drama or a comedy?
¿Se trata de un drama o de una comedia?
Seh trah'-tah deh oon drah'-mah au deh oo'-nah cau-meh'-de-ah?

How long is the interval?
¿Cuánto dura el entreacto?
Coo-ahn'-toh doo'-rah el en-treh-ac'-toh?

104

Ten minutes. If you want, you can go to the hall or to the bar

Diez minutos. Pueden salir al vestíbulo o pasar al bar si lo desean

De-eth' me-noo'-tohs. Poo-eh'-den sah-leer' ahl ves-tee'-boo-loh au pah-sar' ahl bar see loh de-seh'-ahn

CINEMA

Screen	Technicolour	Cinemascope
Pantalla	Tecnicolor	Cinemascope
Pahn-tah'-lyah	*Tec-ne-cau-laur'*	*The-neh-mah-scau'-peh*

Documental	Bill-board	Film
Documental	Cartelera	Película
Dau-coo-men-tahl'	*Cahr-teh-leh'-rah*	*Peh-lee'-coo-lah*

Which film do you recommend me for this evening?

¿Qué película me recomienda para esta tarde?

Keh' peh-lee'-coo-lah meh reh-cau-me-en'-dah pah'-rah es'-tah tar'-deh?

I should like to see a French film

Me gustaría ver alguna película francesa

Meh goos-tah-ree'-ah ver ahl-goo'-nah peh-lee'-coo-lah frahn-the'-sah

The cinema ... is showing a film of ...

En el cina ... dan una película de ...

En el thee'-neh ... dahn oo'-nah peh-lee'-coo-lah deh ...

There is a première in ...

Tiene un estreno en el cine ...

Te-eh'-neh oon es-treh'-noh en el thee'-neh ...

105

Usher, is there an interval?
Acomodador, ¿podría decirme si hay descanso?
Ah-cau-mau-dah-daur', pau-dree'-ah deh-theer'-meh see ah'-e des-cahn'-soh?

Yes, sir, between the documental and the film
Sí, señor, entre el documental y la película
See, seh-nyaur', en'-treh el doh-coo-men-tahl' ee lah peh-lee'-coo-lah

Is the documental a good one?
¿Es bueno el documental?
Es boo-eh'-noh el doh-coo-men-tahl'?

NIGHT CLUBS

Can you recommend me a night club which is not too dear?
¿Puede recomendarme una sala de fiestas que no sea demasiado cara?
Poo-eh'-deh reh-cau-men-dar'-meh oo'-nah sah'-lah deh fe-es'-tas keh no seh'-ah deh-mah-se-ah'-doh cah'-rah?

Take us to a good night club
Llévenos a una buena sala de fiestas
Lyeh'-veh-nohs ah oo'-nah boo-eh'-nah sah'-lah deh fe-es'-tas

Dinner jacket must be worn
El traje de etiqueta es obligatorio
El trah'-he deh eh-te-keh'-tah es au-blee-gah-tau'-reh-oh

A table for two, please
Una mesa para dos, por favor
Oo'-nah meh'-sah pah'-rah daus, paur fah-vaur'

At what time does the show start?
¿A qué hora son las atracciones?
Ah keh' au'-rah saun las ah-trac-the-au'-nes?

What can we have?
¿Qué podemos tomar?
Keh' pau-deh'-mohs tau-mar'?

May I have this dance?
¿Quiere concederme este baile?
Ke-eh'-reh caun-the-der'-meh es'-teh bah'-e-leh?

Are the drinks included?
¿Están incluidas las consumiciones?
Es-tahn' in-cloo-ee'-das las caun-soo-me-the-au'-nes?

How much is it?
¿Qué le debo?
Keh' leh deh'-boh?

Are the tickets numbered?
¿Son numeradas las localidades?
Saun noo-meh-rah'-das las lau-cah-le-dah'-des?

At what time does the session end?
¿A qué hora termina esta sesión?
Ah keh' au'-rah ter-mee'-nah es'-ta seh-se-aun'?

Which bus or underground can I take at the end of the performance?
¿Qué autobús o metro puedo tomar a la salida?
Keh' ah-oo-tau-boos' au meh'-troh poo-eh'-doh tau-mar' ah lah sah-lee'-dah?

THE PROCESS OF A BULLFIGHT

Before the bullfight, in the morning, the bulls are raffled, that is to say, the bulls which belong to each «matador» are drawn out. There are generally six, two for each «matador».

Then comes the «apartado»; that means that each bull gets classified in the «corral», ready to leave it when its turn comes in the afternoon's fight.

The bullfight is divided into the following «thirds», which are signaled by the president of the bullfight by taking out a coloured handkerchief as a signal. At the sight of this handkerchief the band plays some bugle chords:

1. The bull runs out of the pen, spurred by the badge. At the signal of the president, followed by a bugle sound, the «picadors» ride out on their horses. They stab the bull in the fat of its nape to take away some of its strength. According to the ordinances, they must stab it three times.

2. At a new signal or bugle sound, the «picadors» leave and the assistants stick the «banderillas» into the bull. The «matador» can also stick them in, if the wants or knows how to do it. They stick three pairs of «banderillas» into the bull.

3. After doing his «brindis», the «matador» faces the bull with his red flag, making as many passes as he can or judges that are necessary with one hand or both, mastering the bull, until it is ready to be killed.

The bull-ring, the sands	Pen for bulls before the fight	The matador, head of the bull-fighters
La plaza	El toril	El matador
La plah'-tha	*El tau-reel'*	*El mah-tah-dor'*

Cloak of bright colour used by bullfighters	Red flag used by bull-fighters	Short poniard for the finishing stroke
El capote de paseo	La muleta	La puntilla
El cah-poh'-teh deh pah-seh'-oh	*La moo-leh'-tah*	*La poon-tee'-lyah*

Badge, device	Space between the barrier and the public	Troop of bull-fighters under the matador
La divisa	El callejón	La cuadrilla
La de-vee'-sah	*El cah-lyeh-haun'*	*Lah coo-ah-dree'-lyah*

Affixer of special darts into the bull's nape	Cloak used by bullfighters to tire the bull	Banderillas
El banderillero	El capote de faena	Las banderillas
El ban-deh-re-'yeh'-roh	*El cah-poh'-teh deh fah-eh'-nah*	*Las ban-deh-ree'-lyas*

Applause	Presidency	Sheltering barrier for the bullfighters
Los aplausos	La presidencia	El burladero
Lohs ah-plah'-oo-sohs	*Lah preh-se-den'-the-ah*	*El boor-lah-deh'-roh*

Bullfighters	Picador, horseman, armed with a goad	Sword
Los toreros	El picador	La espada, el estoque
Lohs toh-reh'-rohs	*El pee-cah-dor'*	*Lah es-pah'-dah, el es-toh'-keh*

Bullfighter's goad	The bullfighters that help the matador	Whistles
La pica	Los peones	Los pitos
Lah pee'-cah	*Lohs peh-oh'-nes*	*Lohs pee'-tohs*

Rider (constable) that communicates the orders of the presidency
El alguacilillo
El ahl-goo-ah-thee-lee'-lyoh

Give me two inner barrier seats, please (in the shade or in the sun)
Deme dos contrabarreras (tendidos de sol o sombra)
Deh'-meh dohs con-trah-bar-reh'-ras (ten-dee'-dohs deh sohl oh sohm'-brah)

At what time does the fight start?
¿A qué hora empieza la corrida?
Ah keh' oh'-rah em-pe-eh'-thah lah caur-ree'-dah?

Soon the crew will start making the parade
Pronto saldrá la cuadrilla haciendo el paseíllo
Praun'-toh sahl-drah' lah coo-ah-dree'-lyah ah-the-en'-doh el pah-seh-ee'-lyoh

The constable receives the keys from the president in order to start the bullfight
El alguacil recibe del presidente las llaves para que empiece la corrida
El ahl-goo-ah-theel' reh-thee'-beh dehl preh-se-den'-teh las lyah'-ves pah'-rah keh em-pe-eh'-theh lah caur-ree'-dah

The bull will come out when the bugle sounds
El toro saldrá cuando suene el clarín
El tau'-roh sahl-drah' coo-an'-doh soo-eh'-neh el clah-reen'

Will the matador fight with the capote?
¿Va a dar el matador los lances con el capote?
Vah ah dar el mah-tah-daur' lohs lan'-thes caun el cah-pau'-teh?

Yes, now he is fighting the bull by «chicuelinas»
Sí, ahora torea por chicuelinas
See, ah-au'-rah tau-reh'-ah paur che-coo-eh-lee'-nas

What comes after the fight against the goad?
¿Qué viene después de la suerte de varas?
Keh' ve-eh'-neh des-poo-es' deh lah soo-er'-teh deh vah'-ras?

The «banderillero» sticks the «banderillas» into the bull's nape
El banderillero pondrá las banderillas al toro
El ban-deh-re-lyeh'-roh paun-drah' las ban-de-ree'-lyas ahl tau'-roh

What is the meaning of «brindar» the bull?
¿Qué es brindar el toro?
Keh' es brin-dar' el tau'-roh?

The «matador» offers the death of the bull to someone, to the public or to the president
El matador ofrece la muerte del toro a alguna persona, al público o al presidente
El mah-tah-daur' oh-freh'-theh lah moo-er'-teh del tau'-roh ah ahl-goo'-nah per-sau'-nah, ahl poo'-blee-coh auh ahl preh-se-den'-teh

After having tired the bull with the «muleta», the «matador» fits it out to be stabbed
Tras los pases de muleta, el matador pone al toro en suerte de matar
Tras lohs pah'-ses deh moo-leh'-tah, el mah-tah-daur' pau'-neh ahl tau'-roh en soo-er'-teh deh mah-tar'

Has he killed it after a good stab?
¿Lo ha matado de una buena estocada?
Loh ah mah-tah'-doh deh oo'-nah boo-eh'-nah es-tau-cah'-dah?

Yes, the public applaud a lot and wave their handkerchiefs asking for an ear as a prize for the «matador»
Sí, el público aplaude mucho y agita los pañuelos pidiendo la oreja como premio para el torero.
See, el poo'-blee-coh ah-plah'-oo-deh moo'-choh ee ah-hee'-tah lohs pah-nyoo-eh'-lohs pe-de-en'-doh lah au-reh'-hah coh'-moh preh'-me-oh pah'-rah el tau-reh'-roh

ON THE BEACH

Raft
Balsa
Bahl'-sah

Boat
Botc
Boh'-teh

Cabin
Caseta
Cah-seh'-tah

Sand
Arena
Ah-reh'-nah

Sunshade
Sombrilla
Saum-bree'-lyah

Wave
Ola
Oh'-lah

I want to hire a cabin
Deseo alquilar una caseta
Deh-seh'-oh ahl-keeh-lahr' oo'-nah cah-seh'-tah

Are there any showers?
¿Hay duchas?
Ah'-ee doo'-chass?

Where can I hire a boat?
¿Dónde puedo alquilar una canoa?
Daun'-deh poo-eh'-doh ahl-keeh-lahr oo'-nah cah-noh'-ah?

How much is it?
¿Cuánto es?
Coo-ahn'-toh es?

Is it dangerous to swim here?
¿Es peligroso bañarse aquí?
Es peh-leeh-groh'-soh bah-nyahr'-seh ah'-kee?

It is forbidden to swim offshore
Está prohibido alejarse de la orilla
Es-tah' proh-eeh-beeh'-doh ah-leh-hahr'-seh deh lah au-reeh'-lyah

The red flag means danger
La bandera roja indica peligro
Lah bahn-deh'-rah roh'-hah in-deeh'-cah peh-leeh'-groh

The sand is very dirty
La arena está muy sucia
Lah ah-reh'-nah es-tah' moo'-ee' sooh-theah

May we play here?
¿Se puede jugar aquí?
Seh poo-eeh'-deh hoo-gahr' ah'-kee?

No; there is a playing area
No; hay una zona reservada para juegos
No; ah'-ee oo'-nah thau'-nah reh-sehr-vah'-dah pah'-rah hoo-eh'-gohs

SPORTS

Chess	**Mountaine-ering**	**Athletics**
Ajedrez	Alpinismo	Atletismo
Ah-heh-dreth'	*Ahl-peeh-nees'-moh*	*Ah-tleh-tees'-moh*
Basket-ball	**Billiards**	**Boxing**
Baloncesto	Billar	Boxeo
Bah-laun-thehs'-toh	*Bee-lyahr'*	*Bauk-seh'-oh*
Skiing	**Foot-ball**	**Golf**
Esquí	Fútbol	Golf
Es-keeh'	*Foot-baul*	*Gaulf'*
Swimming	**Fishing**	**Tennis**
Natación	Pesca	Tenis
Nah-tah-thee-ohn'	*Pehs'-cah*	*Teh-neehs'*

Is there any foot-ball match?
¿Hay algún partido de fútbol?
Ah'-ee ahl-goon' pahr-tee'-doh deh foot-baul'?

Will it be easy to get tickets?
¿Será fácil conseguir entradas?
Seh-rah' fah'-theel caun-seh-gheer' ehn-trah'-dahs?

CAMPING

Site	**Map**	**Peg**
Terreno	Mapa	Piquete
Tehr-reh'-noh	*Mah'-pah*	*Pe-keh'-teh*
Saucepan	**Tent**	**Lamp**
Cacerola	Tienda	Lámpara
Cah-theh-rau'-lah	*Te-ehn'-dah*	*Lahm-pah'-rah*
Gas	**Air matress**	**Caravan**
Gas	Colchoneta de aire	Remolque
Gas	*Caul-choh-neh'-tah deh ah-ee'-reh*	*Reh-maul'-keh*
Corkscrew	**Tin opener**	**Electric point**
Sacacorchos	Abrelatas	Enchufe
Sah-cah-caur'-chaus	*Ah-breh-lah'-tahs*	*En-chooh'-feh*

Where are the nearest camping sites?
¿Cuáles son los campings más próximos?
Coo-ah'-lehs saun lohs cam-pings mahs' prauk'-seeh-maus?

Is it near the sea? In the mountains?
¿Está en la playa? ¿En la montaña?
Es-tah' en lah plah'-lyah? En lah maun-tah'-nyah?

Which is the camping fee?, per person?
¿Cuánto cuesta la acampada?, ¿por persona?
Coo-ahn'-toh coo-ehs'-tah lah ah-cahm-pah'-dah? paur per-soh'-nah?

What is the car fee? And the caravan?
¿Cuánto paga el automóvil? ¿Y el remolque?
Coo-ahn'-toh pah'-gah el ah-oo-tau-moh'-veel? E el reh-mohl'-keh?

Are there any electric points?, fresh water?
¿Hay tomas eléctricas?, ¿agua potable?
Ah'-ee tau'-mahs eh-lehk'-tree-cas? ah-goo'-ah pau-tah'-bleh?

Where can I do my shopping?
¿Dónde puedo hacer mis compras?
Daun'-deh poo-eh'-doh ah-ther' mees cohm'-pras?

Can we light a fire?
¿Podemos hacer fuego?
Pau-deh'-mohs ah-ther' foo-eh'-goh?

116

SOCIAL RELATIONS

Visiting a country and not meeting its inhabitants is like being a fish on dry land. Approach the Spanish; their natural kindness will be even greater if you make the approach easier by speaking to them in their own language.

My name is ...
Me llamo ...
Meh lyah'-moh ...

How are you?
¿Cómo está usted?
Cau'-moh es-tah' oos-ted'?

Pleased to meet you
Mucho gusto en conocerle
Moo'-choh goos'-toh en cau-nau-ther'-leh

117

This is my wife
Le presento a mi esposa
Leh preh-sen'-toh ah mee es-pau'-sah

Excuse me
Discúlpeme
Des-cool'-peh-meh

It does not matter
No importa
No im-paur'-tah

Do you like it here?
¿Le gusta nuestra ciudad?
Leh goos'-tah noo-es'-trah the-oo-dahd'?

I like it very much
Me ha encantado
Meh ah en-cahn-tah'-doh

May I help you?
¿Le puedo ayudar?
Leh poo-eh'-doh ah-yoo-dar'?

When are you leaving?
¿Hasta cuándo se queda usted?
As'-tah coo-ahn'-doh seh keh'-dah oos-ted'?

I am here for three days (a week, a month)
Estaré tres días (una semana, un mes)
Es-tah-reh' tres dee'-as (oo'-na seh-mah'-nah, oon mes)

Where are you staying?
¿En qué hotel está hospedado?
En keh' au-tel' es-tah' aus-peh-dah'-dôh?

I am staying at ... hotel
Estoy en el hotel ...
Es-toh'-e en el au-tel' ...

118

Would you like a cigarette?
¿Un cigarrillo?
Oon thee-gar-ree'-lyoh?

Very pleased
Con mucho gusto
Caun moo'-choh goos'-toh

Please
Por favor
Paur fah-vaur'

Would you like something to drink?
¿Desea tomar algo?
Deh-seh'-ah tau-mar' ahl'-goh?

Thank you
Gracias
Grah'-the-as

Help yourself
Sírvase usted
Seer'-vah-seh oos-ted'

To your health (cheers!)
¡A su salud!
Ah soo sah-lood!

(With) Best regards
Muchos recuerdos
Moo'-chohs reh-coo-er'-dohs

(Many) Happy returns
Muchas felicidades
Moo'-chas feh-le-thee-dah'-des

Congratulations
Felicidades
Feh-le-thee-dah'-des

119

Merry Christmas!
¡Felices Pascuas!
Feh-lee'-thes pahs'-coo-as!

Happy New Year
¡Feliz Año Nuevo!
Feh-leeth' ah'-nyoh noo-eh'-voh!

Good luck
Buena suerte
Boo-eh'-nah soo-er'-teh

I am sorry
Lo siento
Loh se-en'-toh

May I have the pleasure of this dance?
¿Quiere usted bailar?
Ke-eh'-reh oos-ted' bah-ee-lar'?

Do you want something?
¿Desea algo?
Deh-seh'-ah ahl'-goh?

Do you play tennis?
¿Juega usted al tenis?
Hoo-eh'-gah oos-ted' ahl teh'-nis?

Do you like swimming?
¿Le gusta nadar?
Leh goos'-tah nah-dar'?

What is your address?
¿Cuál es su dirección?
Coo-ahl' es soo de-rec-the-aun'?

Your phone number?
¿Su teléfono?
Soo teh-leh'-fau-noh?

Sit down, please
Siéntese, por favor
Se-en'-teh-seh, paur fah-vaur

We have enjoyed it very much
Nos hemos divertido mucho
Naus eh'-mohs de-ver-tee'-doh moo'-choh

What a beautiful thing!
¡Qué bonito!
Keh' bau-nee'-toh!

It is wonderful!
¡Esto es maravilloso!
Es-toh es mah-rah-ve-lyau'-soh!

It is very sad
Es muy triste
Es moo'-e trees'-teh

What a pity!
¡Qué lástima!
Keh' las'-te-mah!

We shall write to you
Le escribiremos
Leh es-cree-be-reh'-mohs

At your service
Estamos a su disposición
Es-tah'-mohs ah soo dis-pau-se-the-aun'

I do not understand
No comprendo
Nau caum-pren'-doh

Speak slowly, please
Hable usted más despacio, por favor
Ah'-bleh oos-ted' mas des-pah'-the-oh, paur fah-vaur'

Write it, please
Por favor, escríbamelo
Paur fah-vaur', es-cree'-bah-meh-loh

Do you speak French?
¿Habla usted francés?
Ah'-blah oos-ted' frahn-thes'?

THE FAMILY

Grandfather	**Grandmother**	**Grandparents**
Abuelo	Abuela	Abuelos
Ah-boo-eh'-loh	*Ah-boo-eh'-lah*	*Ah-boo-eh'-lohs*
Father	**Mother**	**Parents**
Padre	Madre	Padres
Pah'-dreh	*Mah'-dreh*	*Pah'-dres*
Husband	**Wife**	**Couple**
Marido	Mujer	Esposos
Mah-ree'-doh	*Moo-her'*	*Es-pau'-sohs*
Son	**Daughter**	**Children**
Hijo	Hija	Hijos
Ee'-hoh	*Ee'-hah*	*Ee'-hohs*
Grandson	**Granddaughter**	**Grandchildren**
Nieto	Nieta	Nietos
Ne-eh'-toh	*Ne-eh'-tah*	*Ne-eh'-tohs*
Uncle	**Aunt**	**Cousin**
Tío	Tía	Primo
Tee'-oh	*Tee'-ah*	*Pree'-moh*
Nephew	**Niece**	**Boyfriend**
Sobrino	Sobrina	Novio
Sau-bree'-nòh	*Sau-bree'-nah*	*Nau'-ve-oh*

Girlfriend
Novia
Nau'-ve-ah

Friend
Amigo
Ah-mee'-goh

Brother
Hermano
Er-mah'-noh

Sister
Hermana
Er-mah'-nah

THE TIME

Hour
Hora
Au'-rah

Minute
Minuto
Me-noo'-toh

Second
Segundo
Seh-goon'-doh

Clock
Reloj de pared
Reh-lau' deh pah-red'

Watch
Reloj de pulsera
Reh-lau' deh pool-seh'-rah

It loses
Atrasa
Ah-trah'-sah

It gains
Adelanta
Ah-deh-lahn'-tah

Half an hour
Media hora
Meh'-de-ah au'-rah

Quarter
Cuarto de hora
Coo-ar'-toh deh au'-rah

Noon
Mediodía
Meh-de-oh-dee'-ah

Midnight
Medianoche
Meh-de-ah-nau'-cheh

Morning
Mañana
Mah-nyah'-nah

Afternoon
Tarde
Tar'-deh

Evening
Tarde
Tar'-deh

Night
Noche
Nau'-cheh

What time is it?
¿Qué hora es?
Keh' au'-rah es?

It is five o'clock
Son las cinco
Saun las theen'-coh

124

Ten past three
Las tres y diez
Las tres ee de-eth'

A quarter past two
Las dos y cuarto
Las daus ee coo-ar'-toh

Half past six
Las seis y media
Las seh'-ees ee meh'-de-ah

A quarter to ten
Las diez menos cuarto
Las de-eth' meh'-naus coo-ar'-toh

My watch loses
Mi reloj se atrasa
Mee reh-lau'-seh ah-trah'-sah

My watch gains
Mi reloj adelanta
Mee reh-lau'-ah-deh-lahn'-tah

It is too soon (late)
Es demasiado pronto (tarde)
Es deh-mah-se-ah'-doh praun'-toh (tar'-deh)

It is time to go to bed
Es hora de ir a la cama
Es au'-rah deh eer ah lah cah'-mah

It is time to get up
Es hora de levantarse
Es au'-rah deh leh-vahn-tar'-seh

What time shall I expect you?
¿A qué hora le espero?
Ah keh' au'-rah leh es-peh'-roh?

CALENDAR

Day
Día
Dee'-ah

Week
Semana
Seh-mah'-nah

Month
Mes
Mes

Year
Año
Ah'-nyoh

Century
Siglo
See'-gloh

Today
Hoy
Au'-e

Yesterday

Ayer
Ah-yer'

Tomorrow

Mañana
Mah-nyah'-nah

The day before yesterday

Anteayer
Ahn-teh-ah-yer'

Leap year

Año bisiesto
Ah'-nyoh be-se-es'-toh

Weekly

Semanal
Seh-mah-nahl'

New Year's Day

Año Nuevo
Ah'-nyoh noo-eh'-voh

Good Friday
Viernes Santo
Ve-er'-nes sahn'-toh

Easter
Pascua
Pas'-coo-ah

Whitsuntide
Pentecostés
Pen-teh-caus-tes'

Christmas
Navidad
Nah-ve-dahd'

After tomorrow
Pasado mañana
Pah-sah'-doh mah-nyah'-nah

Monday	Lunes	*Loo'-nes*
Tuesday	Martes	*Mar'-tes*
Wednesday	Miércoles	*Me-er'-cau-les*
Thursday	Jueves	*Hoo-eh'-ves*
Friday	Viernes	*Ve-er'-nes*
Saturday	Sábado	*Sah'-bah-doh*
Sunday	Domingo	*Dau-meen'-goh*

January	Enero	*Eh-neh'-roh*
February	Febrero	*Feh-breh'-roh*
March	Marzo	*Mar'-thoh*
April	Abril	*Ah-breel'*
May	Mayo	*Mah'-yoh*
June	Junio	*Hoo'-ne-oh*
July	Julio	*Hoo'-le-oh*
August	Agosto	*Ah-gaus'-toh*
September	Setiembre	*Seh-te-em'-breh*
October	Octubre	*Auc-too'-breh*
November	Noviembre	*Nau-ve-em'-breh*
December	Diciembre	*De-the-em'-breh*

Spring	Primavera	*Pre-mah-veh'-rah*
Summer	Verano	*Veh-rah'-noh*
Autumn (fall)	Otoño	*Au-tau'-nyoh*
Winter	Invierno	*In-ve-er'-noh*

What is the day today?
¿Qué día es hoy?
Keh' dee'-ah es au'-e?

Last Monday
El lunes pasado
El loo'-nes pah-sah'-doh

Next Thursday
El jueves próximo
El hoo-eh'-ves prauc'-se-moh

The first of March
1 de Marzo
Oo'-noh deh mar'-thoh

The fifteenth of May
15 de Mayo
Keen'-theh deh mah'-yoh

12 of October
12 de Octubre
Dau'-theh deh auc-too'-breh

127

HAIRDRESSER

Hairdresser
Peluquero
Peh-loo-keh'-roh

Scissors
Tijeras
Te-heh'-ras

Brush
Cepillo
Theh-pee'-lyoh

Dryer
Secador
Seh-cah-daur'

Lotion
Loción
Lau-the-aun'

Scalp massage
Masaje
Mah-sah'-heh

Shampooing
Lavado de
cabeza
*Lah-vah'-doh deh
cah-beh'-thah*

Set
Peinado

Pei-nah'-doh

Hair cut
Corte

Caur'-teh

Tinted
Teñido
Teh-nyee'-doh

Permanent
Permanente
Per-mah-nen'-teh

Shave
Afeitar
Ah-fei-tar'

Manicure
Manicura
Mah-ne-coo'-rah

Fringe
Flequillo
Fleh-kee'-lyoh

Parting
Raya
Rah'-yah

LADIES

Where can I find a hairdresser?
¿Dónde hay una peluquería?
Daun'-deh ah'-e oo'-nah peh-loo-keh-ree'-ah?

I want my hair washed and set
Lavar y peinar, por favor
Lah-var' ee peh-e-nar', paur fah-vaur

Shall I cut off a little?
¿Le corto un poco?
Leh caur'-toh oon pau'-coh?

Not too much off the top (sides)
No me deje muy corto de arriba (de los costados)
No meh deh'-heh moo'-e caur'-toh deh ar-ree'-bah (deh lohs caus'-tah'-dohs)

How shall I set your hair?
¿Cómo quiere que le peine?
Cau'-moh ke-eh'-reh keh leh peh'-e-ne?

Towards the back, without any parting
Todo hacia atrás, sin raya
Tau'-doh ah'-the-ah ah-tras', seen rah'-yah

The parting a little higher
Con la raya un poco más alta
Caun lah rah'-yah oon pau'-coh mas ahl'-tah

As you want
Como a usted le parezca
Cau'-moh ah oos-ted' leh pah-reth'-cah

Can you tint my hair?
¿Podría teñirme el pelo?
Pau-dre'-ah teh-nyeer'-meh el peh'-loh?

Same colour?
¿Del mismo color?
Del mees'-moh cau-laur'?

A little darker (lighter)
Un poco más oscuro (claro)
Oon pau'-coh mas aus-coo'-roh (clah'-roh)

The water is too cold (hot)
El agua está demasiado fría (caliente)
El ah'-goo-ah es-tah' deh-mah-se-ah'-doh fre'-ah (cah-le-en'-teh)

I want a manicure
Deseo una manicura
Deh-seh'-oh oo'-nah mah-ne-coo'-rah

Give me the newspaper (a magazine), please
Deme el periódico (una revista), por favor
Deh'-meh el peh-re-au'-de-coh (oo'-nah reh-vees'-tah), paur fah-vaur'

GENTLEMEN

A hair cut and a shave
Un corte de pelo y un afeitado
Oon caur'-teh deh peh'-loh ee oon ah-fei-tah'-doh

Not too short
No demasiado corto
Nau deh-mah-se-ah'-doh caur'-toh

Cut more off the back
Corte más de atrás
Caur'-teh mas deh ah-tras'

Where shall I make the parting?
¿Dónde quiere que le haga la raya?
Daun'-deh ke-eh'-reh keh leh ah'-gah lah rah'-yah?

On the left (right) side
Al lado izquierdo (derecho)
Ahl lah'-doh eeth-ke-er'-doh (deh-reh'-choh)

Do not shave me against the hair
No me afeite a contrapelo
No meh ah-fei'-teh ah caun-trah-peh'-loh

How much is it altogether?
¿Qué le debo por todo?
Keh' leh deh'-boh paur tau'-doh?

My hair is oily (dry)
Tengo el pelo graso (seco)
Ten'-goh el peh'-loh grah'-soh (seh'-coh)

Give me a dandruff lotion, please
Deme una loción contra la caspa
Deh'-me oo'-na lau-the-aun' caun'-trah lah cas'-pah

THE DOCTOR

We hope that you will never have to resort to this place in the GUIDE. But if some difficulty or inconvenience occurs which threatens to embitter your journey, don't hesitate to make use thereof, as it will solve your problem at once.

Doctor	**Ill, sick**	**Temperature**
Doctor	Enfermo	Fiebre
Dauc-taur'	*En'-fer'-moh*	*Fe-eh'-breh*

Pain	**Shivers**	**Cut**
Dolor	Escalofríos	Corte
Dau-laur'	*Es-cah-lau-free'-ohs*	*Caur'-teh*

Bruise	**Burn**	**Wound**
Contusión	Quemadura	Herida
Caun-too-se-aun'	*Keh-mah-doo'-rah*	*Eh-ree'-dah*

Cold	**Indigestion**	**Nausea**
Resfriado	Indigestión	Náuseas
Res-free-ah'-doh	*In-de-hes-te-aun'*	*Nah'-oo-seh-as*

I am ill
Estoy enfermo
Es-tau'-e en-fer'-moh

Call a doctor, please
Llame a un médico, por favor
Lyah'-meh ah oon meh'-de-coh, paur fah-vaur

Where does it hurt?
¿Dónde le duele?
Daun'-deh leh doo-eh'-leh?

I have a pain here
Me duele aquí
Meh doo-eh'-leh ah-kee'

In the head, in the chest
En la cabeza, en el pecho
En lah cah-beh'-thah, en el peh'-choh

I have a temperature
Tengo fiebre
Ten'-goh fe-eh'-breh

133

I have a bad cold
Estoy muy resfriado
Es-tau'-e moo'-e res-free-ah'-doh

I have stomachache after meals
Me duele el estómago después de la comida
Meh doo-eh'-leh el es-tau'-mah-goh des-poo-es' deh lah cau-mee'-dah

Undress, please
Quítese la ropa, por favor
Kee'-teh-seh lah rau'-pah, paur fah-vaur'

Have you had any bad illness?
¿Ha tenido enfermedades graves?
Ah teh-nee'-doh en-fer-meh-dah'-des grah'-ves?

I am allergic, diabetic
Soy alérgico, diabético
Sau'-e ah-ler'-he-coh, de-ah-beh'-te-coh

Breatle, exhale, cough, put out your tongue
Respire, espire, tosa, saque la lengua
Res-pee'-reh, es-pee'-reh, tau'-sah, sah'-keh lah len'-goo-ah

Enough
Ya basta
Yah bas'-tah

How long have you been ill?
¿Desde cuándo está usted enfermo?
Des'-deh coo-ahn'-doh es-tah' oos-ted' en-fer'-moh?

Two days ago
Hace dos días
Ah'-the daus dee'-as

Is it bad? Is it broken?, sprained?
¿Es grave? ¿Está roto?, ¿torcido?
Es grah'-veh? Es-tah' rau'-toh?, taur-thee'-doh?

You must stay in bed for two or three days
Debe quedarse en cama dos o tres días
Deh'-beh keh-dar'-seh en cah'-mah daus au tres dee'-as

I will prescribe you some injections
Voy a recetarle inyecciones
Vau'-e ah reh-theh-tar'-leh in-yec-the-au'-nes

Take these pills every three hours
Tome estas pastillas, una cada tres horas
Tuu'-meh es'-tahs pas-tee'-lyahs, oo'-nah cah'-dah tres au'-rahs

THE DENTIST

Where can I find a dentist?
¿Dónde puedo encontrar un dentista?
Daun'-deh poo-eh'-doh en-caun-trar' oon den-tees'-tah?

This tooth hurts
Me duele este diente, esta muela
Meh doo-eh'-leh es'-teh de-en'-teh, es'-tah moo-eh'-luh

I must extract it
Será preciso sacarla
Seh-rah' preh-thee'-soh sah-car'-lah

Do not extract it. If possible, give me a sedative
No me la saque. Si es posible, deme un calmante
No meh lah sah'-keh. See es pau-see'-bleh, deh'-meh oon cahl-mahn'-teh

135

The filling has fallen out
Se le ha caído el empaste
Seh leh ah cah-ee'-doh el em-pas'-teh

Can you fill it at once?
¿Puede empastármelo en seguida?
Poo-eh'-deh em-pahs-tar'-meh-loh en seh-ghee'-dah?

THE HUMAN BODY

Head	**Ear**	**Eye**
Cabeza	Oreja	Ojo
Cah-beh'-thah	*Au-reh'-hah*	*Au'-hoh*
Nose	**Mouth**	**Eyebrow**
Nariz	Boca	Ceja
Nah-reeth'	*Bau'-cah*	*Theh'-hah*

Eyelashes	**Eyelids**	**Neck**
Pestañas	Párpados	Cuello
Pes-tah'-nyas	*Par'-pah-dohs*	*Coo-eh'-lyoh*
Throat	**Shoulder**	**Arm**
Garganta	Hombro	Brazo
Gar-gahn'-tah	*Aum'-broh*	*Brah'-thoh*
Elbow	**Forearm**	**Hand**
Codo	Antebrazo	Mano
Cau'-doh	*Ahn-teh-brah'-thoh*	*Mah'-noh*
Finger	**Nail**	**Hip**
Dedo	Uña	Cadera
Deh'-doh	*Oo'-nyah*	*Cah-deh'-rah*
Thigh	**Knee**	**Leg**
Muslo	Rodilla	Pierna
Moos'-loh	*Rau-dee'-lyah*	*Pe-er'-nah*
Heart	**Stomach**	**Liver**
Corazón	Estómago	Hígado
Cau-rah-thaun'	*Es-tau'-mah-goh*	*Ee'-gah-doh*
Kidneys	**The vesicle**	**The veins**
Riñones	La vesícula	Las venas
Re-nyau'-nes	*Lah veh-see'-coo-lah*	*Las veh'-nas*
The arteries	**The intestines**	**Ankle**
Las arterias	Los intestinos	Tobillo
Las ar-teh'-re-as	*Lohs in-tes-tee'-nohs*	*Tau-be'-lyoh*

TELEPHONE

Don't be afraid. Perhaps you might need to phone a person who knows English, but beforehand you must cross a small barrier: the secretary, the maid..., somebody, with whom you have to try out your linguistic talents. Then glance at this small chapter and you will find yourself in the best position to overcome such difficulties.

I want to make a call to ...
Quiero telefonear a ...
Keh-eh'-roh teh'-le-fau-neh-ar' ah ...

Operator, get me ...
Señorita, póngame con ...
Seh-nyau-ree'-tah, paun'-gah-meh caun ...

The line is engaged
La línea está ocupada
Lah lee'-neh-ah es-tah' au-coo-pah'-dah

There is no reply
No contestan
Nau caun-tes'-tahn

You have got the wrong number
Se ha equivocado
Seh ah eh-ke-vau-cah'-doh

You have the wrong number
Ha marcado mal
Ah mar-cah'-doh mahl

Ring again
Vuelva a llamar
Voo-el'-vah ah lyah-mar'

Who is speaking?
¿Con quién hablo?
Caun ke-en' ah'-bloh?

I am Mr ... I want to speak to Mr ...
Soy el Sr ..., quisiera hablar con el Sr ...
*Sau'-e el seh-nyaur' ..., ke-se-eh'-rah ah-blar' caun el
seh-nyaur' ...*

Hold the line
No cuelgue
No coo-el'-gheh

He is out
Ha salido
Ah sah-lee'-doh

At what time will he be back?
¿A qué hora volverá?
Ah keh' au'-rah vaul-veh-rah'?

At what number can I reach him?
¿A qué número puedo llamarle?
Ah keh noo'-meh-roh poo-eh'-doh lyah-mar'-leh?

Ring number ...
Marque el número ...
Mar'-keh el noo'-meh-roh ...

Will you take a message?
¿Quiere usted tomar un recado?
Ke-eh'-reh oos-ted' tau-mar' oon reh-cah'-doh?

Tell him that Mr ... has called
Dígale que ha llamado el Sr ...
Dee'-gah-leh keh ah lyah-mah'-doh el seh-nyaur' ...

Ask him to call me, number ...
Dígale que me llame al número ...
Dee'-gah-leh keh meh lyah'-meh ahl noo'-meh-roh ...

I will be in town until Saturday
Estaré en la ciudad hasta el sábado
Es-tah-reh' en la the-oo-dahd' as'-tah el sah'-bah-doh

THE POST OFFICE

Letter	Stamp	Pillar box
Carta	Sello	Buzón
Car'-tah	*Seh'-lyoh*	*Boo-thaun'*
Postcard	**Poste restante**	**Business papers**
Tarjeta postal	Lista de correos	Papeles de negocios
Tar-heh'-tah paus-tahl'	*Lees'-tah deh caur-reh'-ohs*	*Pah-peh'-les deh neh-gau'-the-ohs*
Post office	**Telegram**	**Window**
Correos	Telegrama	Ventanilla
Caur-reh'-ohs	*Teh-leh-grah'-mah*	*Ven-tah-nee'-lyah*

Urgent
Urgente
Oor-hen'-teh

Parcel post
Paquete postal
Pah-keh'-teh
paus-tahl'

Word
Palabra
Pah-lah'-brah

Address

Dirección
De-rec-the-aun'

Excess amount
Sobretasa
Sau-breh-tah'-sah

Envelope

Sobre
Sau'-breh

Sealing-wax
Lacre
Lah'-creh

The post office, please
¿Para ir a Correos, por favor?
Pah'-rah eer ah caur-reh'-ohs, paur fah-vaur'?

Put a stamp on this letter
Franquee esta carta
Frahn-keh'-eh es'-tah car'-tah

What is the postage for a registered letter?
¿Cuál es el franqueo de una carta certificada?
Coo-ahl' es el frahn-keh'-oh deh oo'-nah car'-tah ther-te-fe-cah'-dah?

What is the postage to England?
¿Cuál es el franqueo para Inglaterra?
Coo-ahl' es el frahn-keh'-oh pah'-rah in-glah-ter'-rah?

And the air mail postage?
¿Y el franqueo por avión?
Ee el frahn-keh'-oh paur ah-ve-aun'?

Please register this letter
Sírvase certificar esta carta
Seer'-vah-seh ther-te-fe-car' es'-tah car'-tah

Please seal this letter
Sírvase lacrar esta carta
Seer'-vah-seh lah-crar' es'-tah car'-tah

Where is the telegram office?
¿Dónde está el servicio de Telégrafos?
Daun'-deh es-tah' el ser-vee'-the-oh deh teh-leh'-grah-fohs?

How much is it per word?
¿Cuánto cuesta una palabra?
Coo-ahn'-toh coo-es'-tah oo'-nah pah-lah'-brah?

I want to send this parcel by post
Quiero enviar este paquete postal
Ke-eh'-roh en-ve-ar' es'-teh pah-keh'-teh paus-tahl'

Do you want it insured?, registered?
¿Desea usted asegurarlo?, ¿certificarlo?
Deh-seh'-ah oos-ted' ah-seh-goo-rar'-loh?, ther-te-fe-car'-loh?

Is there any letter for me at the poste restante?
¿Hay carta para mí en la lista de correos?
Ah'-e car'-tah pah'-rah mee en lah lees'-tah deh caur-reh'-ohs?

What documents do I need to collect a package?
¿Qué documentos necesito para retirar un paquete postal?
Keh' dau-coo-men'-tohs neh-the-see'-toh pah'-rah reh-te-rar' oon pah-keh'-teh paus-tahl'?

Your passport will be enough
Basta con su pasaporte
Bas'-tah caun soo pah-sah-paur'-teh

THE BANK

Where can I change my money?
Por favor, ¿para cambiar moneda?
Paur fah-vaur', pah'-rah cahm-be-ar' mau-neh'-dah?

Counter number ...
Ventanilla número ...
Ven-tah-nee'-lyah noo'-meh'-roh ...

What is the rate for the peseta?
¿Cuál es el cambio de la peseta?
Coo-ahl' es el cahm'-be-oh deh lah peh-seh'-tah?

Your documents, please
Sus documentos, por favor
Soos dau-coo-men'-tohs, paur fah-vaur'

Sign here
Firme aquí
Feer'-meh ah-kee'

143

Can you change this traveller's cheque?
¿Puede cambiarme este cheque de viajero?
Poo-eh'-deh cahm-be-ar'-meh es'-teh cheh'-keh deh ve-ah'-heh'-roh?

Give me change in coins, please
Por favor, deme moneda fraccionaria
Paur fa-vaur', deh'-meh mau-neh'-dah frac-the-au-nah'-re-ah

Have you received a transfer from ...?
¿Podría decirme si han recibido una transferencia de ...?
Pau-dree'-ah deh-theer'-meh see ahn reh-the-bee'-doh oo'-nah trans-feh-ren'-the-ah deh ...?

Addressed to ...
A nombre de ...
Ah naum'-breh deh ...

Not yet, sir
Aún no, señor
Ah-oon' no, seh-nyaur'

Can I cash this bearer cheque?
¿Puedo cobrar este cheque al portador?
Poo-eh'-doh cau-brar' es'-teh cheh'-keh ahl paur-tah-daur'?

We do not take personal cheques
No aceptamos cheques de particulares
No ah-thep-tah'-mohs cheh'-kehs deh pahr-te-coo-lah'-res

Go to the cash counter, please
Pase a caja, por favor
Pah'-seh ah cah'-hah, paur fah-vaur'

Give me small notes
Deme billetes pequeños
Deh'-meh bee-lye'-tes peh-keh'-nyos

144

PUBLIC OFFICES

Cabinet

Ministerio
Me-nees-teh'-re-oh

Court

Juzgado
Hooth-gah'-doh

County council

Diputación
De-poo-tah-the-aun'

Town hall

Alcaldía
Ahl-cahl-dee'-ah

Police station

Comisaría
Cau-me-sah-ree'-ah

Cathedral

Catedral
Cah-teh-drahl'

Church

Iglesia
E-ghleh'-se-ah

Chapel

Capilla
Cah-pee'-lyah

Palace

Palacio
Pah-lah'-the-oh

Castle

Castillo

Cas-tee'-lyoh

Bishopric

Obispado

Au-bees-pah'-doh

Fine Arts Museum

Museo de Bellas Artes

Moo-seh'-oh deh beh'-lyahs ar-tes

Post office

Correos

Caur-reh'-ohs

Stock exchange

Bolsa

Baul'-sah

Chamber of Commerce

Cámara de Comercio

Cah'-mah-rah deh cau-mer'-the-oh

THE REPORT

Police	Mugging	Embassy
Policía	Atraco	Embajada
Pau-lee-thee'-ah	*Ah-trah'-coh*	*Em-bah-hah'-dah*

Police Station	Swindle	Passport
Comisaría	Estafa	Pasaporte
Cau-me-sah-ree'-ah	*Es-tah'-fah*	*Pah-sah-paur'-teh*

Police Officer	Handbag	Lawyer
Agente de policía	Bolso	Abogado
Ah-hen'-teh deh	*Baul'-soh*	*Ah-bau-gah'-doh*
pau-lee-thee'-ah		

Theft	Wallet	Process
Robo	Cartera	Trámite
Rau'-boh	*Car-teh'-rah*	*Trah'-me-teh*

I want to report to the police that I have been robbed, mugged, swindled..., etc.

¿Quiero hacer una denuncia, porque me han robado, atracado, estafado..., etc.

Ke-eh'-roh ah-ther'oo'-nah deh-noon'-thee-ah, paur'-keh meh ahn rau-bah'-doh, ah-trah-cah'-doh, es-tah-fah'-doh, etc.

What is the police telephone number?

¿Cuál es el número de teléfono de la policía?

Coo-ahl' es ehl noo'-meh-roh deh teh-leh'-fau-noh deh lah pau-lee-thee'-ah?

Where is the nearest police station?

¿Dónde está la comisaría más próxima?

Daun'-deh es-tah' lah cau-me-sah-ree'-ah mas prauc'-se-mah?

Taxi, take me to the nearest police station

Taxi, lléveme a la comisaría más cercana

Taxi, lyeh'-veh-meh ah lah cau-me-sah-ree'-ah mas ther-cah'-nah

Officer, I have come to report a ...

Agente, vengo a poner una denuncia

Ah-hen'-teh vehn-goh au pau-ner' oo'-nah deh-noon'-thee-ah

146

I have been the victim of a swindle
He sido víctima de una estafa
Eh see'-doh veec'-te-mah deh oo'-nah es-tah'-fah

My handbag/wallet has been stolen
Me han robado el bolso/la cartera
Meh ahn rau-bah'-doh ehl baul'-soh/lah car-teh'-rah

I have been assaulted
Me han golpeado
Meh ahn gaul-peh-ah'-doh

My passport has disappeared
Me ha desaparecido el pasaporte
Meh ah deh-sah-pah-reh-thee'-doh ehl pah-sah-paur'-teh

I have been overcharged in the restaurant
Me han cobrado de más en el restaurante
Meh ahn cau-brah'-doh deh mas en ehl res-tah-oo-rahn'-teh

I have had a car accident
He tenido un accidente de automóvil
Eh teh-nee'-doh oon ac-se-dehn'-teh deh ah-oo-tau-mau'-veel

How should I fill out the report?
¿Cómo debo cumplimentar la denuncia?
Cau'-moh deh'-boh coom-plee-mehn-tar' lah deh-noon'-thee-ah?

What procedures do I have to go through?
¿Qué trámites debo seguir?
Keh trah'-me-tehs deh-boh seh-gheer'?

Should I consult a lawyer?
¿Debo consultar a un abogado?
Deh'-boh caun-sool-tar' oon ah-bau-gah'-doh?

Should I go to my embassy?
¿Debo acudir a mi embajada?
Deh'-boh ah-coo-deer' ah mee ehm-bah-hah'-dah?

Is it a very complicated process?
¿Se trata de un trámite muy complicado?
Seh trah'-tah deh oon trah'-me-teh moo'-e caum-plee-cah'-doh?

ENGLISH-SPANISH DICTIONARY

Absent. Ausente. *Ah'-oo-sen'-teh*

Absent-minded. Distraído. *Dis-trah-ee'-doh*

Absolute. Absoluto. *Ab-sau-loo'-toh*

Absolutely. Absolutamente. *Ab-sau-loo-tah-men'-teh*

Academy. Academia. *Ah-cah-deh'-me-ah*

Accent. Acento. *Ah-then'-toh*

Accept. Aceptar. *Ah-thep-tar'*

Accident. Accidente. *Ac-se-dehn'-teh*

Accompany. Acompañar. *Ah-caum-pah-nyar'*

Ache. Dolor. *Dau-laur'*

Active. Activo. *Ac-tee'-voh*

Actor. Actor. *Ac-taur'*

Add. Sumar. *Soo-mar'*

Addres. Señas. *Seh'-nyas*

Adhesive tape. Cinta adhesiva. *Theen'-tah ah-deh-see'-vah*

Adjective. Adjetivo. *Ad-heh-tee'-voh*

Admiral. Almirante. *Ahl-me-rahn'-teh*

Admiration. Admiración. *Ad-me-rah-the-aun'*

Admit. Admitir. *Ad-me-teer'*

Adorable. Adorable. *Ah-dau-rah'-bleh*

Advance. Avance. *Ah-vahn'-theh*

Advertisement. Anuncio. *Ah-noon'-the-oh*

Advice. Consejo. *Caun-seh'-hoh*

Affectionate. Afectuoso. *Ah-fec-too-au'-soh*

Age. Edad. *Eh-dahd'*

Agent. Agente. *Ah-hen'-teh*

Air. Aire. *Ah'-e-reh*

Alarm. Alarma. *Ah-lar'-mah*

Alarm clock. Despertador. *Des-per'tah-daur'*

Alcohol. Alcohol. *Ahl-cau-aul'*

Allow. Permitir. *Per-me-teer'*

Almond. Almendra. *Ahl-men'-drah*

Alphabet. Alfabeto. *Ahl-fah-beh'-toh*

Altar. Altar. *Ahl-tar'*

Always. Siempre. *Se-em'-preh*

Ambulance. Ambulancia. *Ahm-boo-lahn'-the-ah*

Amusement. Distracción. *Dis-trac-the-aun'*

Ancient. Antiguo. *Ahn-tee'-goo-oh*

Angel. Ángel. *Ahn'-hel*

Angry. Enojado. *Eh-nau-hah'doh*

Animal. Animal. *Ah-ne-mahl'*

Announcer. Locutor. *Lau-coo-taur'*

Answer. Contestación; responder. *Caun-tes-tah-the-aun'; res-paun-der'*

Anvil. Yunque. *Yoon'-keh*

Anxious. Ansioso. *Ahn-se-au'-soh*

Appointment. Cita. *Thee'-tah*

Appreciate. Apreciar. *Ah-preh-the-ar'*

Arch. Arco. *Ar'-coh*

Archbishop. Arzobispo. *Ar-thau-bees'-poh*

Architect. Arquitecto. *Ar-ke-tec'-toh*

Argue. Disputar. *Dis-poo-tar'*

Army. Ejército. *Eh-her'-the-toh*

Around. Alrededor. *Ahl-reh-deh-daur'*

Arrival. Llegada. *Lyeh-gah'-dah*

Art. Arte. *Ar'-teh*

Artificial. Artificial. *Ar-te-fe-the-ahl'*

Artist. Artista. *Ar-tees'-tah*

Ashamed. Avergonzado. *Ah-ver-gaun-thah'-doh*

Ashtray. Cenicero. *The-ne-theh'-roh*

Assist. Ayudar. *Ah-yoo-dar'*

Attach. Unir; incautar. *Oo-neer'; in-cah-oo-tar'*

Attend. Asistir. *Ah-sis-teer'*

Attendant. Encargado. *En-car-gah'-doh*

Authority. Autoridad. *Ah-oo-tau-re-dahd'*

Available. Disponible. *Dis-pau-nee'-bleh*

Avoid. Evitar. *Eh-ve-tar'*

Awake. Despierto. *Des-pe-er'-toh*

Baby. Nene. *Neh'-neh*

Bad. Mal, malo. *Mahl, mah'-loh*

Bag. Maletín. *Mah-leh-teen'*

Balcony. Balcón. *Bahl-caun'*

Ball point pen. Bolígrafo. *Bau-lee'-grah-foh*

Bandage. Vendaje. *Ven-dah'-heh*

Bathe. Bañar. *Bah-nyar'*

Battery. Pila. *Pee'-lah*

Battle. Batalla. *Bah-tah'-lyah*

Bay. Bahía. *Bah-ee'-ah*

Be. Ser. *Ser*

Beach. Playa. *Plah'-yah*

Beacon. Faro. *Fah'-roh*

Bean. Alubia. *Ah-looh'-be-ah*

Bear. Oso. *Au'-soh*

Beard. Barba. *Bar'-bah*

Beauty. Belleza. *Beh-lyeh'-thah*

Bed. Cama. *Cah'-mah*

Bedroom. Dormitorio. *Daur-me-tau'-re-oh*

Beech-tree. Haya. *Ah'-yah*

Beer. Cerveza. *Ther-veh'-thah*

Beetroot. Remolacha. *Reh-mau-lah'-chah*

Before. Antes. *Ahn'-tes*

Beggar. Mendigo. *Men-dee'-goh*

Begin. Empezar. *Em-peh-thar'*

Believe. Creer. *Creh-er'*

Bell. Campana. *Cahm-pah'-nah*

Belong. Pertenecer. *Per-teh-neh-ther'*

Belt. Cinturón. *Thin-too-raun'*

Bicycle. Bicicleta. *Be-the-cleh'-tah*

Bird. Pájaro. *Pah'-hah-roh*

Birthday. Cumpleaños. *Coom-pleh-ah'-nyohs*

Biscuit. Galleta. *Gah-lyeh'-tah*

Bite. Mordisco; morder. *Maur-dees'-coh; maur-der'*

Bitter. Amargo. *Ah-mar'-goh*

Blind. Ciego. *The-eh'-goh*

Blond. Rubio. *Roo'-be-oh*

Blood. Sangre. *Sahn'-greh*

Blow. Soplar; golpe. *Sau-plar'; gaul'-peh*

Boarding-house. Pensión. *Pen-se-aun'*

149

Boil. Hervir. *Er-veer'*
Bone. Hueso. *Oo-eh'-soh*
Border. Frontera. *Fraun-teh'-rah*
Born (to be). Nacer. *Nah-ther'*
Both. Ambos. *Ahm'-bohs*
Bother. Molestar. *Mau-les-tar'*
Bottle. Botella. *Bau-teh'-lyah*
Bottom. Fondo. *Faun'-doh*
Box. Caja. *Cah'-hah*
Boy. Muchacho. *Moo-chah'-choh*
Bra. Sostén. *Saus-ten'*
Bracelet. Pulsera. *Pool'-seh'-rah*
Brain. Cerebro. *Theh-reh'-broh*
Brake. Freno. *Freh'-noh*
Brave. Valiente. *Vah-le-en'-teh*
Break. Romper. *Raum-per'*
Breakdown. Avería. *Ah-veh-ree'-ah*
Breakwater. Rompeolas. *Raum-peh-au'-las*
Breath. Respiración. *Res-pe-rah-the-aun'*
Bride. Novia. *Nau'-ve-ah*
Bridge. Puente. *Poo-en'-teh*
Bring. Traer. *Trah-er'*
Broom. Escoba. *Es-cau'-bah*
Brush. Cepillo; cepillar. *Theh-pee'-lyioh; theh-pe-lyar'*
Build. Construir. *Cauns-troo-eer'*
Building. Edificio. *Eh-de-fee'-the-oh*
Bulb. Bombilla. *Baum-bee'-lyah*
Bull. Toro. *Tau'-roh*
Bunk. Litera. *Le-teh'-rah*
Burn. Quemar. *Keh-mar'*

Business. Negocio. *Neh-gau'-the-oh*
Businessman. Comerciante. *Cau-mer-the-ahn'-teh*
Butter. Mantequilla. *Mahn-teh-kee'-lyah*
Button. Botón. *Bau-taun'*
Buttonhole. Ojal. *Au-hahl'*
Buy. Comprar. *Caum-prar'*

Cabin. Camarote. *Cah-mah-rau'-teh*
Cable. Cable. *Cah'-bleh*
Cake. Tarta. *Tar'-tah*
Calendar. Calendario. *Cah-len-dah'-re-oh*
Call. Llamar. *Lyah-mar'*
Camp. Acampar. *Ah-cahm-par'*
Can opener. Abrelatas. *Ah-bre-lah'-tas*
Canal. Canal. *Cah-nahl'*
Cap. Gorra. *Gaur'-rah*
Card. Naipe. *Nah'-e-peh*
Carrot. Zanahoria. *Thah-nah-au'-re-ah*
Castle. Castillo. *Cas-tee'-lyoh*
Cat. Gato. *Gah'-toh*
Catalogue. Catálogo. *Cah-tah'-lau-goh*
Catholic. Católico. *Cah-tau'-le-coh*
Cattle. Ganado. *Gah-nah'-doh*
Cellar. Sótano. *Sau'-tah-noh*
Cemetery. Cementerio. *Theh-men-teh'-re-oh*
Century. Siglo. *See'-gloh*
Certain. Cierto. *The-er'-toh*
Chair. Silla. *See'-lyah*
Champagne. Champaña. *Chahm-pah'-nyah*

150

Change. Cambio. *Cahm'-be-oh*

Chapel. Capilla. *Cah-pee'-lyah*

Chesterfield. Gabán. *Gah-bahn'*

Chewing-gum. Chicle. *Chee'-cleh*

Chicken. Pollo. *Pau'-lyoh*

China. Porcelana. *Paur-theh-lah'-nah*

Chocolate. Chocolate. *Chau-cau-lah'-teh*

Choice. Elección. *Eh-lec-the-aun'*

Christian. Cristiano. *Cris-te-ah'-noh*

Church. Iglesia. *E-gleh'-se-ah*

Cider. Sidra. *See'-drah*

Circle. Círculo. *Theer'-coo-loh*

Clamp. Grapa. *Grah'-pah*

Clean. Limpio. *Leem'-pe-oh*

Clerk. Escribiente. *Es-cre-be-en'-teh*

Cloakroom. Guardarropa. *Goo-ar-dar-rau'-pah*

Cloth. Tela. *Teh-lah*

Clothing. Ropa. *Rau'-pah*

Cloud. Nube. *Noo'-beh*

Coal. Carbón. *Car-baun'*

Coast. Costa. *Caus'-tah*

Coat. Abrigo; chaqueta. *Ah-bree'-goh; chah-keh'-tah*

Coat-hanger. Percha. *Per'-chah*

Cock. Gallo; grifo. *Gah'-lyoh; gree'-foh*

Cockroach. Cucaracha. *Coo-cah-rah'-chah*

Cold. Frío; catarro. *Free'-oh; cah-tur'-roh*

Collision. Choque. *Chau'-keh*

Colourless. Incoloro. *In-cau-lau'-roh*

Comb. Peine. *Peh'-e-neh*

Come down. Bajar. *Bah-har'*

Comfort. Comodidad. *Cau-mau-de-dahd'*

Command. Mandar. *Mahn-dar'*

Common. Común. *Cau-moon'*

Communist. Comunista. *Cau-moo-nees'-tah*

Company. Compañía. *Caum-pah-nyee'-ah*

Comparison. Comparación. *Caum-pah-rah-the-aun'*

Compass. Brújula. *Broo'-hoo-lah*

Condition. Condición. *Caun-de-the-aun'*

Confused. Confuso. *Caun-foo'-soh*

Congress. Congreso. *Caun-greh'-soh*

Consider. Considerar. *Caun-se-deh-rar'*

Consonant. Consonante. *Caun-sau-nahn'-teh*

Constipation. Estreñimiento. *Es-treh-nye-me-en'-toh*

Consul. Cónsul. *Caun'-sool*

Contain. Contener. *Caun-teh-ner'*

Continue. Continuar. *Caun-te-noo-ar'*

Conversation. Conversación. *Caun-ver-sah-the-aun'*

Cook. Guisar. *Ghe-sar'*

Copy. Copia. *Cau'-peh-ah*

Cork. Corcho. *Caur'-choh*

Corn. Grano; maíz; trigo. *Grah'-noh; mah-eeth'; tree'-goh*

Corner. Esquina. *Es-kee'-nah*

Corridor. Pasillo. *Pah-see'-lyoh*

Cotton. Algodón. *Ahl-gau-daun'*

Cough. Tos. *Taus*

Count. Contar. *Caun-tar'*

Counter. Mostrador. *Maus-trah-daur'*

Country. Campo; patria; país. *Cahm'-poh; pah'-tre-ah; pah-ees'*

Coupling. Empalme. *Em-pahl'-meh*

Court. Patio; tribunal. *Pah'-te-oh; tre-boo-nahl'*

Courteousness. Urbanidad. *Oor-bah-ne-dahd'*

Cover. Tapa; cubrir. *Tah'-pah; coo-breer'*

Cow. Vaca. *Vah'-cah*

Crab. Cangrejo. *Cahn-greh'-hoh*

Crazy. Loco. *Lau'-coh*

Cream. Crema; pomada. *Creh'-mah; pau-mah'-dah*

Cross. Cruz; cruzar. *Crooth; croo-thar'*

Cry. Gritar; llorar. *Gre-tar'; lyau-rar'*

Cupboard. Armario. *Ar-mah'-re-oh*

Curling iron. Rizador. *Re-thah-daur'*

Custom. Costumbre. *Caus-toom'-breh*

Customs officer. Aduanero. *Ah-doo-ah-neh'-roh*

Cut. Cortar. *Caur-tar'*

Damage. Daño. *Dah'-nyoh*

Dance. Baile; bailar. *Bah'-e-leh; bah-e-lar'*

Danger. Peligro. *Peh-lee'-groh*

Dark. Oscuro. *Aus-coo'-roh*

Dead. Muerto. *Moo-er'-toh*

Debt. Deuda. *Deh'-oo-dah*

Deceive. Engañar. *En-gah-nyar'*

Decide. Decidir. *Deh-the-deer'*

Declare. Declarar. *Deh-clah-rar'*

Deep. Profundo. *Prau-foon'-doh*

Delay. Demora. *Deh-mau'-rah*

Deliver. Entregar; librar. *En-treh-gar'; le-brar'*

Democracy. Democracia. *Deh-mau-crah'-the-ah*

Deny. Negar. *Neh-gar'*

Deposit. Depósito; depositar. *Deh-pau'-se-toh; deh-pau-se-tar'*

Describe. Describir. *Des-cre-beer'*

Desert. Desierto. *Deh-se-er'-toh*

Detail. Detalle. *Deh-tah'-lyeh*

Develop. Desarrollar; revelar fotos. *Des-ar-rau-lyar'; reh-veh-lar' fau'-tosh*

Devil. Diablo. *De-ah'-bloh*

Diamond. Diamante. *De-ah-mahn'-teh*

Diarrhoea. Diarrea. *De-ar-reh'-ah*

Dictionary. Diccionario. *Dic-the-au-nah'-re-oh*

Die. Morir. *Mau-reer'*

Difference. Diferencia. *De-feh-ren'-the-ah*

Different. Diferente. *De-feh-ren'-teh*

Difficult. Difícil. *De-fee'-theel*

Dimension. Dimensión. *De-men-se-aun'*

Dinner. Comida. *Cau-mee'-dah*

152

Dinning-room. Comedor. *Cau-meh-daur'*

Direct. Dirigir; directo. *De-re-heer'; de-rec'-toh*

Director. Director. *De-rec-taur'*

Dirty. Sucio. *Soo'-the-oh*

Disablement. Invalidez. *In-vah-le-deth'*

Disappointment. Desengaño. *Des-en-gah'-nyoh*

Discount. Descuento; rebaja. *Des-coo-en'-toh; reh-bah'-hah*

Dismiss. Despedir. *Des-peh-deer'*

Displease. Disgustar. *Dis-goos-tar'*

Distribution. Distribución. *Dis-tre-boo-the-aun'*

District. Distrito; barrio. *Dis-tree'-toh; bar'-re-oh*

Divide. Dividir. *De-ve-deer'*

Divorce. Divorcio. *De-vaur'-the-oh*

Doctor. Doctor. *Dauc-taur'*

Document. Documento. *Dau-coo-men'-toh*

Dog. Perro. *Per'-roh*

Doll. Muñeca. *Moo-nyeh'-cah*

Donkey. Burro. *Boor'-roh*

Door. Puerta. *Poo-er'-tah*

Doorman. Portero. *Paur-teh'-roh*

Dose. Dosis. *Dau'-sis*

Double. Doble. *Dau'-bleh.*

Dove. Paloma. *Pah-lau'-mah*

Down. Abajo. *Ah-bah'-hoh*

Drain. Desagüe. *Des-ah'-goo-eh*

Draw. Dibujar; sacar. *De-boo-har'; sah-car'*

Drawer. Cajón. *Cah-haun'*

Dress. Traje; vestir. *Trah'-heh; ves-teer'*

Dressmaker. Modista. *Mau-dees'-tah*

Drink. Beber. *Beh-ber'*

Drive. Conducir. *Caun-doo-theer'*

Drop. Gota. *Gau'-tah*

Drugstore. Farmacia. *Far-mah'-the-ah*

Dry. Seco. *Seh'-coh*

Dust. Polvo. *Paul'-voh*

Dye. Teñir. *Teh-nyeer'*

Ear. Oreja. *Au-reh'-hah*

Early. Temprano. *Tem-prah'-noh*

Earrings. Pendientes. *Pen-de-en'-tes*

Easy. Fácil. *Fah'-theel*

Education. Educación. *Eh-doo-cah-the-aun'*

Effect. Efecto. *Eh-fec'-toh*

Elastic. Elástico. *Eh-las'-te-coh*

Electricity. Electricidad. *Eh-lec-tre-the-dahd'*

Elephant. Elefante. *Eh-leh-fahn'-teh*

Embark. Embarcar. *Em-bar-car'*

Embassy. Embajada. *Ehm-bah-hah'-dah*

Emerald. Esmeralda. *Es-meh-rahl'-dah*

Emotion. Emoción. *Eh-mau-the-aun'*

Emperor. Emperador. *Em-peh-rah-daur'*

Employee. Empleado. *Em-pleh-ah'-doh*

Empty. Vacío. *Vah-thee'-oh*

153

End. Fin. *Feen*

Enemy. Enemigo. *Eh-neh-mee'-goh*

Energy. Energía. *Eh-ner-hee'-ah*

Enjoy. Divertirse. *De-ver-teer'-seh*

Entirely. Enteramente. *En-teh-rah-men'-teh*

Equal. Igual. *E-goo-ahl'*

Equipment. Equipo. *Eh-kee'-poh*

Error. Error. *Er-raur'*

Examination. Examen. *Ek-sah'-men*

Example. Ejemplo. *Eh-hem'-ploh*

Excellent. Excelente. *Ex-theh-len'-teh*

Except. Exceptuar; excepto. *Ex-thep-too-ar'; ex-thep'-to*

Excursion. Excursión. *Ex-coor-se-aun'*

Excuse. Excusa; excusar. *Ex-coo'-sah; ex-coo-sar'*

Exercise. Ejercicio. *Eh-her-thee'-the-oh*

Exhibition. Exposición. *Ex-pau-se-thee-aun'*

Expenses. Gastos. *Gas'-tohs*

Explain. Explicar. *Ex-ple-car'*

Export. Exportar. *Ex-paur-tar'*

Express. Expreso. *Ex-preh'-soh*

Eye. Ojo. *Au'-hoh*

Face. Cara. *Cah'-rah*

Factory. Fábrica. *Fah'-bre-cah*

Faint. Desmayarse. *Des-mah-yar'-seh*

Fall. Caer. *Cah-er'*

False. Falso. *Fahl'-soh*

Family. Familia. *Fah-mee'-le-ah*

Fan. Abanico; ventilador; aficionado. *Ah-bah-nee'-coh; ven-te-lah-daur'; ah-fe-the-au-nah'-doh*

Far. Lejos. *Leh'-hohs*

Fashion. Moda. *Mau'-dah*

Fat. Gordo. *Gaur'-doh*

Fault. Culpa. *Cool'-pah*

Fear. Miedo. *Me-eh'-doh*

Female. Hembra. *Em'-brah*

Field. Campo. *Cahm'-poh*

Fig. Higo. *Ee'-goh*

Fill. Llenar. *Lyeh-nar'*

Filling station. Surtidor de gasolina. *Soor-te-daur' deh gah-sau-lee'-nah*

Film. Película. *Peh-lee'-coo-lah*

Find. Encontrar. *En-caun-trar'*

Fine. Hermoso; multa. *Er-mau'-soh; mool-tah*

Finger. Dedo. *Deh'-doh*

Finish. Concluir, acabar. *Caun-cloo-eer', ah-cah-bar'*

Fire. Fuego. *Foo-eh'-goh*

First aid kit. Botiquín. *Bau-te-keen'*

Fish bone. Espina. *Es-pee'-nah*

Fixed. Fijo. *Fee'-hoh*

Flame. Llama. *Lyah'-mah*

Flash. Relámpago; fogonazo. *Reh-lahm'-pah-goh; fau-gau-nah'-thoh*

Flavour. Sabor. *Sah-baur'*

Flight. Vuelo; huída. *Voo-eh'-loh; oo-ee'-dah*

Flood. Inundación. *E-noon-dah-the-aun'*

Floor. Piso; suelo. *Pee'-soh; soo-eh'-loh*

154

Flower. Flor. *Flaur*

Fly. Volar; mosca. *Voh-lar'; maus'cah*

Fog. Niebla. *Ne-eh'-blah*

Follow. Seguir. *Seh-gheer'*

Food. Alimento. *Ah-le-men'-toh*

Forbidden. Prohibido. *Prau-e-bee'-doh*

Foreigner. Extranjero. *Ex-trahn-heh'-roh*

Forget. Olvidar. *Aul-ve-dar'*

Former. Anterior. *Ahn-teh-re-aur'*

Formula. Fórmula. *Faur-moo-lah*

Fortunately. Afortunadamente. *Ah-faur-too-nah-dah-men'-teh*

Fountain. Fuente. *Foo-en'-teh*

Fox. Zorro. *Thaur'-roh*

Free. Libre. *Lee'-breh*

Freight. Flete; carga. *Fleh'-teh; car'-gah*

Frequently. Frecuentemente. *Freh-coo-en-teh-men'-teh*

Fried. Frito. *Free'-toh*

Friend. Amigo. *Ah-mee'-goh*

Frighten. Asustar. *Ah-soos-tar'*

Frog. Rana. *Rah'-nah*

Frozen. Congelado. *Caun-heh-lah'-doh*

Fruit. Fruta. *Froo'-tah*

Frying pan. Sartén. *Sar-ten'*

Funeral. Funeral; entierro. *Foo-neh-rahl'; en-te-er'roh*

Funny. Cómico; divertido. *Cau'-me-coh; de-ver-tee'-doh*

Furniture. Mobiliario. *Mau-be-le-ah'-re-oh*

Future. Futuro. *Foo-too'-roh*

Gala. Gala. *Gah'-lah*

Galaxy. Galaxia. *Gah-lac'-se-ah*

Gallery. Galería. *Gah-leh-ree'-ah*

Gallon. Galón. *Gah-laun'*

Game. Juego. *Hoo-eh'-goh*

Garbage. Basura. *Bah-soo'-rah*

Garden. Jardín. *Har-deen'*

Garlic. Ajo. *Ah'-hoh*

Garter. Liga. *Lee'-gah*

Gas. Gas. *Gas*

Gay. Alegre. *Ah-leh'-greh*

Generous. Generoso. *Heh-neh-rau'-soh*

Gentleman. Caballero. *Cah-bah-lyeh'-roh*

Geography. Geografía. *Heh-au-grah-fee'-ah*

Get. Alcanzar; obtener. *Ahl-cahn-thar'; aub-teh-ner'*

Get dark. Anochecer. *Ah-nau-cheh-ther*

Get fat. Engordar. *En-gaur-dar'*

Get up. Levantarse. *Leh-vahn-tar'-seh*

Get up early. Madrugar. *Mah-droo-gar'*

Ghost. Fantasma; espíritu. *Fahn-tas'-mah; es-pee'-re-too*

Gift. Regalo. *Reh-gah'-loh*

Gin. Ginebra. *He-neh'-brah*

Girl. Muchacha. *Moo-chah'-chah*

Glass. Vaso; cristal. *Vah'-soh; crees-tahl'*

Glasses. Gafas. *Gah'-fas*

Go. Ir. *Eer*

Go away. Marchar. *Mar-char'*

Go out. Salir. *Sah-leer'*

155

Go to bed. Acostarse. *Ah-caus-tar'-seh*

God. Dios. *De-aus'*

Goldsmith. Orfebre. *Aur-feh'-breh*

Good-looking. Guapo. *Goo-ah'-poh*

Government. Gobierno. *Gau-be-er'-noh*

Grape. Uva. *Oo'-vah*

Grass. Hierba. *E-er'-bah*

Grave. Sepulcro. *Seh-pool'-croh*

Grease. Grasa. *Grah'-sah*

Guaranteed. Garantizado. *Gah-rahn-te-thah'-doh*

Guitar. Guitarra. *Ghe-tar'-rah*

Gun. Arma de fuego. *Ar'-mah deh foo-eh'-goh*

Hair. Cabello. *Cah-beh'-lyoh*

Ham. Jamón. *Hah-maun'*

Hammer. Martillo. *Mar-tee'-lyoh*

Hand basin. Lavabo. *Lah-vah'-boh*

Handbag. Bolso. *Baul'-soh*

Handkerchief. Pañuelo. *Pah-nyoo-eh'-loh*

Handle. Manivela. *Mah-ne-veh'-lah*

Hank. Madeja. *Mah-deh'-hah*

Happy. Dichoso; feliz. *De-chau'-soh; feh-leeth*

Hard. Duro. *Doo'-roh*

Hat. Sombrero. *Saum-breh'-roh*

Hate. Odiar. *Au-de-ar'*

Have. Haber; tener; tomar. *Ah-ber'; teh-ner'; tau-mar'*

Have lunch. Almorzar. *Ahl-maur-thar'*

Haversack. Mochila. *Mau-chee'-lah*

Head. Cabeza. *Cah-beh'-thah*

Health. Salud. *Sah-lood'*

Hear. Oir. *Au-eer'*

Heart. Corazón. *Cau-rah-thaun'*

Heat. Calor; calentar. *Cah-laur'; cah-len-tar'*

Heel. Talón. *Tah-laun'*

Hell. Infierno. *In-fe-er'-noh*

Help. Socorro; ayudar. *Sau-caur'-roh; ah-yoo-dar'*

Hen. Gallina. *Gah-lyee'-nah*

Heritage. Herencia. *Eh-ren'-the-ah*

Hero. Héroe. *Eh'-rau-eh*

Hierarchy. Jerarquía. *Heh-rar-kee'-ah*

High. Alto. *Ahl'-toh*

Hill. Colina. *Cau-lee'-nah*

Hoist. Izar. *E-thar'*

Hole. Agujero. *Ah-goo-heh'-roh*

Home. Hogar; patria. *Au-gar; pah'-tre-ah*

Homicide. Homicida. *Au-me-thee'-dah*

Homonymous. Homónimo. *Au-mau'-ne-moh*

Honest. Honrado. *Aun-rah'-doh*

Honey. Miel. *Me-el'*

Honorary. Honorario. *Au-nau-rah'-re-oh*

Honour. Honor. *Au-naur'*

Hope. Esperanza. *Es-peh-rahn'-thah*

Horizontal. Horizontal. *Au-re-thaun-tahl'*

Horn. Cuerno; bocina. *Coo-er'-no; bau-thee'nah*

Horse. Caballo. *Cah-bah'-lyoh*

Hospital. Hospital. *Aus-pe-tahl'*

Hospitality. Hospitalidad. *Aus-pe-tah-le-dahd'*

Hot. Caliente. *Cah-le-en'-teh*

House. Casa. *Cah'-sah*

Human. Humano. *Oo-mah'-noh*

Hunger. Hambre. *Ahm'-breh*

Hunting. Caza. *Cah'-thah*

Hurricane. Huracán. *Oo rah-cahn'*

Ice. Hielo. *E-eh'-loh*

Ice-cream. Helado. *Eh-lah'-doh*

Idea. Idea. *E-deh'-ah*

Identification. Identificación. *E-den-te-fe-cah-the-aun'*

Idiot. Idiota. *E-de-au'-tah*

Ill. Enfermo. *En-fer'-moh*

Illegal. Ilegal. *E-leh-gahl'*

Illustration. Ilustración. *E-loos-trah-the-aun'*

Imagination. Imaginación. *E-mah-he-nah-the-aun'*

Immigration. Inmigración. *In-me-grah-the-aun'*

Incident. Incidente. *In-the-den'-teh*

Included. Incluido. *In-clooee'-doh*

Incomplete. Incompleto. *In-caum-pleh'-toh*

Indemnity. Indemnización. *In-dem-ne-thah-the-aun'*

Independence. Independencia. *In-deh-pen-den'-the-ah*

Indigestion. Indigestión. *In-de-hes-te-aun'*

Individual. Individuo. *In-de-ve'-doo-oh*

Infectious. Contagioso. *Caun-tah-he-au'-soh*

Influenza. Gripe. *Gree'-peh*

Inhabitant. Habitante. *Ah-be-tahn'-teh*

Injection. Inyección. *In-yec-the-aun'*

Ink. Tinta. *Teen'-tah*

Innocent. Inocente. *E-nau-then'-teh*

Insect. Insecto. *In-sec'-toh*

Inside. Dentro. *Den'-troh*

Insist. Insistir. *In-sis-teer'*

Inspect. Inspeccionar. *Ins-pec-the-au-nar'*

Insure. Asegurar. *Ah-seh-goo-rar'*

Intellectual. Intelectual. *In-teh-lec-too-ahl'*

Intelligent. Inteligente. *In-teh-le-hen'-teh*

Intense. Intenso. *In-ten'-soh*

Interpret. Interpretar. *In-ter-preh-tar'*

Interval. Entreacto. *En-treh-ahc'-toh*

Interview. Entrevista. *En-treh-vees'-tah*

Invader. Invasor. *In-vah-saur'*

Inventory. Inventario. *In-ven-tah'-reh-oh*

Investigate. Investigar. *In-ves-te-gar'*

Iodine. Yodo. *Yau'-doh*

Iris. Iris. *Ee'-ris*

Iron. Hierro. *E-er'-roh*

Irony. Ironía. *E-rau-nee'-ah*

Irritate. Irritar. *Eer-re-tar'*

Island. Isla. *Ees'-lah*

Jacket. Chaqueta. *Chah-keh'-tah*

Jail. Cárcel. *Car'-thel*

Jewel. Joya. *Hau'-yah*
Job. Empleo. *Em-pleh'-oh*
Joke. Broma. *Brau'-mah*
Joy. Alegría. *Ah-leh-gree'-ah*
Judge. Juez. *Hoo-eth'*
Judgement. Juicio. *Hoo-ee'-the-oh*
Juice. Jugo. *Hoo'-goh*
Jump. Saltar. *Sahl-tar'*
Jungle. Selva. *Sel'-vah*
Just. Justo. *Hoos'-toh*
Justice. Justicia. *Hoos-tee'-the-ah*

Keep. Guardar. *Goo-ar-dar'*
Key. Llave. *Lyah'-veh*
Kill. Matar. *Mah-tar'*
Kilocycle. Kilociclo. *Ke-loh-thee'cloh*
Kilogram. Kilogamo. *Ke-loh-grah'-moh*
Kilowatt. Kilovatio. *Ke-loh-vah'-te-oh*
Kimono. Kimono. *Ke-mau'-noh*
Kind. Amable; género. *Ah-mah'-bleh; heh'-neh-roh*
King. Rey. *Reh'-e*
Kiosk. Kiosco. *Ke-aus'-coh*
Kiss. Beso. *Beh'-soh*
Knee. Rodilla. *Rau-dee'-lyah*
Knife. Cuchillo. *Coo-chee'-lyoh*
Know. Saber; conocer. *Sah-ber'; cau-nau-ther'*

Label. Etiqueta. *Eh-te-keh'-tah*
Labour. Labor. *Lah-baur'*
Labyrinth. Laberinto. *Lah-beh-reen'-toh*

Lace. Encaje. *En-cah'-heh*
Lady. Dama. *Dah'-mah*
Lake. Lago. *Lah'-goh*
Lamp. Lámpara. *Lahm'-pah-rah*
Land. Tierra; aterrizar. *Te-er'-rah; ah-ter-re-thar'*
Language. Idioma. *E-de-au'-mah*
Last name. Apellido. *Ah-peh-lyee'-doh*
Last night. Anoche. *Ah-nau'-cheh*
Latin. Latino. *Lah-tee'-noh*
Latin-American. Latinoamericano. *Lah-tee'-noh-ah-meh-re-cah'-noh*
Laugh. Reír. *Reh-eer'*
Laundry. Lavandería. *Lah-vahn-deh-ree'-ah*
Law. Ley. *Leh'-e*
Lawyer. Abogado. *Ah-bau-gah'-doh*
Laxative. Laxante. *Lac-sahn'-teh*
Lazy. Perezoso. *Peh-reh-thau'-soh*
Lead. Plomo. *Plau'-moh*
Leader. Jefe; guía; sedal. *Heh'-feh; ghee'-ah; seh-dahl'*
Leaf. Hoja. *Au'-hah*
Leak. Escape; fuga. *Es-cah'-pe; foo'-gah*
Learn. Aprender. *Ah-prender'*
Leather. Cuero. *Coo-eh'-roh*
Leave. Dejar. *Deh-har'*
Lecture. Conferencia. *Caun-feh-ren'-the-ah*
Left-handed. Zurdo. *Thoor-doh*
Legend. Leyenda. *Leh-yen'-dah*

Lemon. Limón. *Le-maun'*

Lemonade. Limonada. *Le mau-nah'-dah*

Lesson. Lección. *Lec-the-aun'*

Letter. Carta. *Car'-tah*

Letter box. Buzón. *Boo-thaun'*

Lettuce. Lechuga. *Leh-choo'-gah*

Liberty. Libertad. *Le-ber-tahd'*

Library. Biblioteca. *Be-ble-au-teh'-cah*

Licence. Licencia. *Le-then'-the-ah*

Lie. Mentir; yacer. *Men-teer'; yah-ther'*

Life-jacket. Salvavidas. *Sahl-vah-vee'-das*

Lift. Ascensor. *As-then-saur'*

Light. Luz; encender; ligero. *Looth; en-then-der'; le-heh'-roh*

Lighter. Encendedor. *En-then-deh-daur'*

Like. Gustar. *Goos-tar'*

Limit. Límite. *Lee'-me-teh*

Linen. Lino; ropa blanca. *Lee'-noh; rau'-pah blahn'-cah*

Lion. León. *Leh-aun'*

Lip. Labio. *Lah'-be-oh*

Liquor. Licor. *Le-caur'*

List. Lista. *Lees'-tah*

Listen. Escuchar. *Es-coo-char'*

Little. Poco; pequeño. *Pau'-coh; peh-keh'-nyoh*

Live. Vivir. *Ve-veer'*

Lizard. Lagarto. *Lah-gar'-toh*

Load. Carga. *Car'-gah*

Lobster. Bogavante. *Boh-gah-vahn'-teh*

Lock. Cerradura. *Ther-rah-doo'-rah*

Locomotive. Locomotora. *Lau-cau-mau-tau'-rah*

Lodging. Alojamiento. *Ah-lau-hah-me-en'-toh*

Look. Mirar. *Me-rar'*

Look for. Buscar. *Boos-car'*

Loose. Flojo. *Flau'-hoh*

Lost. Perdido. *Per-dee'-doh*

Love. Amor; amar. *Ah-maur'; ah-mar'*

Luck. Suerte. *Soo-er'-teh*

Lunch. Almuerzo. *Ahl-moo-er'-thoh*

Lung. Pulmón. *Pool-maun'*

Luxurious. Lujoso. *Loo-hau'-soh*

Magnet. Imán. *E-mahn'*

Magnificent. Magnífico. *Mag-nee'-fe-coh*

Maid. Criada. *Cre-ah'-dah*

Majority. Mayoría. *Mah-yau-ree'-ah*

Make. Hacer. *Ah-ther'*

Man. Hombre. *Aum'-breh*

Manager. Gerente. *Heh-ren'-teh*

Marble. Mármol. *Mar'-maul*

Mare. Yegua. *Yeh'-goo-ah*

Mark. Marca. *Mar'-cah*

Market. Mercado. *Mer-cah'-doh*

Marquis. Marqués. *Mar-kes'*

Married. Casado. *Cah-sah'-doh*

Mass. Masa; misa. *Mah'-sah; mee'-sah*

Match. Cerilla. *Theh-ree'-lyah*

Material. Material. *Mah-teh-re-ahl'*

Mattress. Colchón. *Caul-chaun'*

159

Mausoleum. Mausoleo. *Mah-oo-sau-leh'-oh*

Mayor. Alcalde. *Ahl-cahl'-deh*

Meal. Comida. *Cau-mee'-dah*

Measure. Medida. *Meh-dee'-dah*

Medicine. Medicina. *Meh-de-thee'-nah*

Meet. Encontrar. *En-caun-trar'*

Meeting. Reunión. *Reh-oo-ne-aun'*

Member. Miembro. *Me-em'-broh*

Message. Mensaje. *Men-sah'-heh*

Metal. Metal. *Meh-tahl'*

Milk. Leche. *Leh'-cheh*

Mirror. Espejo. *Es-peh'-hoh*

Misfortune. Desgracia. *Des-grah'-the-ah*

Missionary. Misionero. *Me-se-au-neh'-roh*

Mistake. Equivocación; error. *Eh-ke-vau-cah-teh-aun'; er-raur'*

Mixed. Mezclado. *Meth-clah'-doh*

Molecule. Molécula. *Mau-leh'-coo-lah*

Money. Dinero. *De-neh'-roh*

Monkey. Mono. *Mau'-noh*

Monument. Monumento. *Mau-noo-men'-toh*

Moon. Luna. *Loo'-nah*

Mosaic. Mosaico. *Mau-sah'-e-coh*

Mosque. Mezquita. *Meth-kee'-tah*

Mother of pearl. Nácar. *Nah'-car*

Mother-in-law. Suegra. *Soo-eh'-grah*

Mount. Monte. *Maun'-teh*

Mountain. Montaña. *Maun-tah'-nyah*

Mourning. Duelo; luto. *Doo-eh'-loh; loo'-toh*

Mouse. Ratón. *Rah-taun'*

Mud. Fango. *Fahn'-goh*

Mugging. Atraco. *Ah-trah'-coh*

Murder. Asesino. *Ah-seh-see'-noh*

Muscle. Músculo. *Moos'-coo-loh*

Mushroom. Hongo. *Aun'-goh*

Musician. Músico. *Moo'-se-coh*

Must. Deber. *Deh-ber'*

Mustache. Bigote. *Be-gau'-teh*

Mustard. Mostaza. *Maus-tah'-thah*

Naked. Desnudo. *Des-noo'-doh*

Nap. Siesta. *Se-es'-tah*

Napkin. Servilleta. *Ser-ve-lyeh'-tah*

Narrow. Estrecho. *Es-treh'-choh*

Native. Nativo. *Nah-tee'-voh*

Nature. Naturaleza. *Nah-too-rah-leh'-thah*

Nausea. Náusea. *Nah'-oo-seh-ah*

Need. Necesidad; necesitar. *Neh-theh-se-dahd'; neh-the-se-tar'*

Needle. Aguja. *Ah-goo'-hah*

Neighbour. Vecino. *Veh-thee'-noh*

Nephew. Sobrino. *Sau-bree'-noh*

Nephritis. Nefritis. *Neh-free'-tis*

Nerve. Nervio. *Ner'-ve-oh*

Net. Red. *Red*

New. Nuevo. *Noo-eh'-voh*

News. Noticias. *Nau-tee'-the-ahs*

Newspaper. Diario. *De-ah'-re-oh*

Next. Inmediato; próximo. *In-meh-de-ah'-toh; prauc'-se-moh*

Niece. Sobrina. *Sau-bree'-nah*

Noise. Ruido. *Roo-ee'-doh*

Nonsense. Disparate. *Dis-pah-rah'-teh*

North. Norte. *Naur'-teh*

Notebook. Cuaderno. *Coo-ah-der'-noh*

Nothing. Nada. *Nah'-dah*

Novel. Novela. *Nau-veh'-lah*

Novelty. Novedad. *Nau-veh-dahd'*

Now. Ahora. *Ah-au'-rah*

Numismatic. Numismática. *Noo-mis-mah'-te-cah*

Nuptial. Nupcial. *Noop-the-ahl'*

Nurse. Enfermera. *En-fer-meh'-rah*

Oasis. Oasis. *Au-ah'-sis*

Obedience. Obediencia. *Au-beh-de-en'-the-ah*

Object. Objeto. *Aub-heh'-toh*

Oblique. Oblicuo. *Au-blee'-coo-oh*

Observatory. Observatorio. *Aub-ser-vah-tau'-re-oh*

Obtain. Obtener. *Aub-teh-ner'*

Obvious. Obvio. *Aub'-ve-oh*

Occasion. Ocasión. *Au-cah-se-aun'*

Ocean. Océano. *Au-theh'-ah-noh*

Oil. Aceite, petróleo. *Ah-thei'-teh; peh-trau'-leh-oh*

Olive. Aceituna. *Ah-thei-too'-nah*

Onion. Cebolla. *Theh-bau'-lyah*

Open. Abrir. *Ah-breer'*

Operating theatre. Quirófano. *Ke-rau'-fah-noh*

Opposite. Opuesto. *Au-poo-es'-toh*

Optician. Óptico. *Aup'-te-coh*

Orchid. Orquídea. *Aur-kee'-deh-ah*

Organ. Órgano. *Aur'-gah-noh*

Out of order. Descompuesto. *Des-caum-poo-es'-toh*

Oven. Horno. *Aur'-noh*

Overcoat. Gabán. *Gah-bahn'*

Overturn. Volcar. *Vaul-car'*

Owl. Búho. *Boo'-oh*

Owner. Propietario. *Prau-pe-eh-tah'-reh-oh*

Oxide. Óxido. *Auc'-se-doh*

Oxygen. Oxígeno. *Auc-see'-heh-noh*

Oyster. Ostra. *Aus'-trah*

Pack of cards. Baraja. *Bah-rah'-hah*

Package. Paquete. *Pah-keh'-teh*

Packing. Embalaje. *Em-bah-lah'-heh*

Page. Página. *Pah'-he-nah*

Pain. Dolor. *Dau-laur'*

Painting. Pintura. *Pin-too'-rah*

161

Pair. Pareja. *Pah-reh'-hah*

Pajamas. Pijama. *Pe-hah'-mah*

Palace. Palacio. *Pah-lah'-the-oh*

Pale. Pálido. *Pah'-le-doh*

Palm tree. Palmera. *Pahl-meh'-rah*

Panties. Bragas. *Brah'-gas*

Paper. Papel. *Pah-pel'*

Parallel. Paralelo. *Pah-rah-leh'-loh*

Parsley. Perejil. *Peh-reh-heel'*

Partition wall. Tabique. *Tah-bee'-keh*

Party. Fiesta; reunión. *Fe-es'-tah; reh-oo-ne-aun'*

Passage. Pasaje. *Pah-sah'-heh*

Passport. Pasaporte. *Pah-sah-paur'-teh*

Pastry. Pastel. *Pas-tel'*

Patient. Paciente; enfermo. *Pah-the-en'-teh; en-fer'-moh*

Patrol. Patrulla. *Pah-troo'-lyah*

Pavement. Acera. *Ah-theh'-rah*

Pavilion. Pabellón. *Pah-beh-lyaun'*

Paw. Zarpa. *Thar'-pah*

Peace. Paz. *Path*

Peanut. Cacahuete. *Cah-cah-oo-eh'-teh*

Pearl. Perla. *Per'-lah*

Pearly. Nacarado. *Nah-cah-rah'-doh*

Peasant. Campesino. *Cahm-peh-see'-noh*

Pebble. Guijarro. *Ghe-har'-roh*

Pedestrian. Peatón. *Peh-ah-taun'*

Pen. Pluma. *Ploo'-mah*

Pencil. Lápiz. *Lah'-pith*

Penitence. Penitencia. *Peh-ne-ten'-the-ah*

People. Gente. *Hen'-teh*

Pepper. Pimienta. *Pe-me-en'-tah*

Performance. Representación; actuación. *Reh-preh-sen-tah-the-aun'; ac-too-ah-the-aun'*

Perspiration. Sudor. *Soo-daur'*

Petticoat. Enaguas. *Eh-nah'-goo-as*

Pick up. Recoger. *Reh-cau-her'*

Picture. Cuadro; retrato. *Coo-ah'-droh; reh-trah'-toh*

Pier. Muelle; malecón. *Moo-eh'-lyeh; mah-leh-caun'*

Pig. Cerdo. *Ther'-doh*

Pilgrim. Peregrino. *Peh-reh-gree'-noh*

Pill. Píldora; pastilla. *Peel'-dau-rah; pas-tee'-lyah*

Pillow. Almohada. *Ahl-mau-ah'-dah*

Pilot. Piloto. *Pe-lau'-toh*

Pin. Alfiler. *Ahl-fe-ler'*

Piping. Tubería. *Too-beh-ree'-ah*

Pistol. Pistola. *Pis-tau'-lah*

Pit-coal. Hulla. *Oo'-lyah*

Place. Lugar. *Loo-gar'*

Plain. Llano; llanura. *Lyah'-noh; lyah-noo'-rah*

Play. Jugar. *Hoo-gar'*

Pleasant. Agradable. *Ah-grah-dah'-ble*

Pneumonia. Neumonía. *Neh-oo-mau-nee'-ah*

Pocket. Bolsillo. *Baul-see'-lyoh*

Poem. Poema. *Pau-eh'-mah*

162

Poison. Veneno. *Veh-neh'-noh*

Police Station. Comisaría. *Cau-me-sah-ree'-ah*

Policeman. Policía. *Pau-le-thee'-ah*

Pool. Piscina. *Pis-thee'-nah*

Poor. Pobre. *Pau'-breh*

Port. Babor; puerto. *Bah-baur'; poo-er'-toh*

Postman. Cartero. *Car-teh'-roh*

Postpone. Aplazar. *Ah-plah-thar'*

Pound. Libra. *Lee'-brah*

Powder. Polvo; pólvora. *Paul'-voh; paul'-vau-rah*

Power. Potencia; poder. *Pau-ten'-the-ah; pau-der'*

Prawn. Gamba. *Gahm'-bah*

Prayer. Oración. *Au-rah-the-aun'*

Precious. Precioso. *Preh-the-au'-soh*

Prescription. Receta. *Reh-theh'-tah*

Present. Regalo; presente. *Reh-gah'-loh; pre-sen'-teh*

Pressing-iron. Plancha (ropa). *Plahn'-chah*

Pretty. Bonito. *Bau-nee'-toh*

Priest. Cura; sacerdote. *Coo'-ra; sah-ther-dau'-teh*

Prisoner. Prisionero. *Pre-se-au-neh'-roh*

Prizer. Premio. *Preh'-me-oh*

Process. Trámite. *Trah'-me-teh*

Professor. Profesor. *Prau-feh-saur'*

Profit. Beneficio. *Beh-neh-fe'-the-oh*

Properly. Debidamente. *Deh-be-dah-men'-teh*

Protection. Protección. *Prau-tec-the-aun'*

Proud. Orgulloso. *Aur-goo-lyau'-soh*

Province. Provincia. *Prau-veen'-the-ah*

Pull out. Sacar. *Sah-car'*

Punish. Castigar. *Cas-te-gar'*

Pure. Puro. *Poo'-roh*

Push. Empujar. *Em-poo-har'*

Put. Poner. *Pau-ner'*

Put in. Meter. *Meh-ter'*

Quality. Calidad. *Cah-le-dahd'*

Quantity. Cantidad. *Cahn-te-dahd'*

Queen. Reina. *Rei'-nah*

Quickly. Rápidamente. *Rah-pe-dah-men'-teh*

Rabbit. Conejo. *Cau-neh'-hoh*

Race. Raza. *Rah'-thah*

Radioactivity. Radiactividad. *Rah-de-ahc-te-ve-dahd'*

Radish. Rábano. *Rah'-bah-noh*

Rage. Rabia. *Rah'-be-ah*

Rain. Lluvia; llover. *Lyoo'-ve-ah; lyau-ver*

Raincoat. Impermeable; gabardina. *Im-per-meh-ah'-ble; gah-bar-dee'-nah*

Rat. Rata. *Rah'-tah*

Ray. Rayo. *Rah'-yoh*

Reach. Alcanzar. *Ahl-cahn-thar'*

Read. Leer. *Leh-er'*

Reason. Razón. *Rah-thaun'*

Receipt. Recibo. *Reh-thee'-boh*

163

Receive. Recibir. *Reh-the-beer'*

Reconcile. Reconciliar. *Reh-caun-the-le-ar'*

Record. Disco. *Dees'-coh*

Recover. Recobrar. *Reh-cau-brar'*

Red Cross. Cruz Roja. *Crooth' rau'-hah*

Reduction. Reducción; rebaja. *Reh-dooc-the-aun'; reh-bah'-hah*

Reef. Escollo. *Es-cau'-lyoh*

Referee. Árbitro. *Ar'-be-troh*

Refreshment. Refresco. *Reh-fres'-coh*

Refrigerator. Nevera. *Neh-veh'-rah*

Refund. Reembolso. *Reh-em-baul'-soh*

Refuse. Rehusar. *Reh-oo-sar'*

Regard. Saludo. *Sah-loo'-doh*

Regimen. Régimen. *Reh'-he-men*

Region. Región. *Reh-he-aun'*

Registration number. Matrícula. *Mah-tree'-coo-lah*

Regret. Lamentar. *Lah-men-tar'*

Regulation. Regulación. *Reh-goo-lah-the-aun'*

Remain. Permanecer. *Per-mah-neh-ther'*

Remember. Recordar. *Reh-caur-dar'*

Remove. Quitar. *Ke-tar'*

Rent. Alquilar. *Ahl-ke-lar'*

Repair. Reparar. *Reh-pah-rar'*

Repeat. Repetir. *Reh-peh-teer'*

Reply. Respuesta; replicar. *Res-poo-es'-tah; reh-plee-car'*

Report. Denunciar. *Deh-noon-thee-ahr'*

Reporter. Reportero. *Reh-paur-teh'-roh*

Representative. Representante. *Reh-preh-sen-tahn'-teh*

Responsibility. Responsabilidad. *Res-paun-sah-be-le-dahd'*

Rest. Descanso; descansar. *Des-cahn'-soh; des-cahn-sar'*

Return. Volver. *Vaul-ver'*

Reveal. Revelar. *Reh-veh-lar'*

Review. Revista. *Reh-vees'-tah*

Rib. Costilla. *Caus-tee'-lyah*

Rich. Rico. *Ree'-coh*

Rights. Derechos. *Deh-reh'-chohs*

Ring. Anillo. *Ah-nee'-lyoh*

River. Río. *Ree'-oh*

Roast. Asado. *Ah-sah'-doh*

Rock. Roca. *Rau'-cah*

Roller. Rulo. *Roo'-loh*

Roof. Tejado. *Teh-hah'-doh*

Room. Habitación. *Ah-be-tah-the-aun'*

Rope. Cuerda. *Coo-er'-dah*

Rough. Áspero. *As'-peh-roh*

Round. Redondo. *Reh-daun'-doh*

Rubber. Caucho; goma. *Cah'-oo-cho; gau'-mah*

Ruby. Rubí. *Roo-bee'*

Rude. Grosero. *Grau-seh'-roh*

Rug. Alfombra. *Ahl-faum'-brah*

Ruin. Ruina. *Roo-ee'-nah*

Russia. Rusia. *Roo'-se-ah*

Sad. Triste. *Trees'-teh*

Saddle. Silla de montar. *See'-lyah deh maun-tar'*

Safety-pin. Imperdible. *Im-per-dee'-bleh*

Sale. Venta. *Ven'-tah*

Salesman. Vendedor. *Ven-deh-daur'*

Salt. Sal. *Sahl*

Sand. Arena. *Ah-reh'-nah*

Sapphire. Zafiro. *Thah-fee'-roh*

Sauce. Salsa. *Sahl'-sah*

Sausage. Salchicha. *Sahl-chee'-chah*

Saw. Sierra. *Se-er'-rah*

Say. Decir. *Deh-theer'*

Scales. Balanza. *Bah-lahn'-tha*

Scarce. Escaso. *Es-cah'-soh*

Scarf. Bufanda. *Boo-fahn'-dah*

School. Escuela. *Es-coo-eh'-lah*

Science. Ciencia. *The-en'-teh-ah*

Scissors. Tijeras. *Te-heh'-ras*

Scotch. Escocés. *Es-cau-thes'*

Scratch. Rasguño. *Ras-goo'-nyoh*

Screw. Tornillo. *Taur-nee'-lyoh*

Sea. Mar. *Mar*

Sealing wax. Lacre. *Lah'-creh*

Seat. Asiento. *Ah-se-en'-toh*

Secret. Secreto. *Seh-creh'-toh*

Seduction. Seducción. *Seh-dooc-the-aun'*

See. Ver. *Ver*

Seem. Parecer. *Pah-reh-ther'*

Send. Enviar. *En-ve-ar'*

Serve. Servir. *Ser-veer'*

Sew. Coser. *Cau-ser'*

Shade. Sombra. *Saum'-brah*

Shampoo. Champú. *Chahm-poo'*

Shark. Tiburón. *Te-boo-raun'*

Sharp. Agudo. *Ah-goo'-doh*

Shave. Afeitar. *Ah-fei-tar'*

Sheep. Oveja. *Au-veh'-hah*

Sheet. Sábana. *Sah'-bah-nah*

Sherry. Jerez. *Heh-reth'*

Shock absorber. Amortiguador *Ah-maur-te-goo-ah-daur'*

Shop. Tienda. *Te-en'-dah*

Shop assistant. Dependiente. *Deh-pen-de-en'-teh*

Shop window. Escaparate. *Es-cah-pah-rah'-teh*

Shot. Disparo. *Dis-pah'-roh*

Shoulder. Hombro. *Aum'-broh*

Shout. Grito; gritar. *Gree'-toh; gre-tar'*

Show. Espectáculo; mostrar. *Es-pec-tah'-coo-loh; maus-trar'*

Shower. Ducha. *Doo'-chah*

Shutter. Persiana. *Per-se-ah'-nah*

Sickness. Enfermedad. *En-fer-meh-dahd'*

Sign. Letrero; firmar. *Leh-treh'-roh; feer-mar'*

Signal. Señal. *Seh-nyahl'*

Silence. Silencio. *Se-len'-the-oh*

Silk. Seda. *Seh'-dah*

Silver. Plata. *Plah'-tah*

Similar. Similar. *Se-me-lar'*

Sincere. Sincero. *Sin-the'-roh*

Sing. Cantar. *Cahn-tar'*

Single. Único. *Oo'-ne-coh*

Sink. Hundir. *Oon-deer'*

Sky. Cielo. *The-eh'-loh*

Skyscraper. Rascacielos. *Ras-cah-the-eh'-lohs*

Sleep. Dormir. *Daur-meer'*

Sleeve. Manga. *Mahn'-gah*

Slipper. Zapatilla. *Thah-pah-tee'-lyah*

165

Slippery. Resbaladizo. *Resbah-lah-dee'-thoh*

Slow. Lento. *Len'-toh*

Smell. Oler. *Au-ler'*

Smile. Sonrisa; sonreír. *Saunree'-sah; saun-reh-eer'*

Smoke. Humo; fumar. *Oo'-moh; foo-mar'*

Smooth. Liso; suave. *Lee'-soh; soo-ah'-veh*

Snail. Caracol. *Cah-rahcaul'*

Snake. Culebra. *Coo-leh'-brah*

Snow. Nieve. *Ne-eh'-veh*

Soap. Jabón. *Hah-baun'*

Soldier. Soldado. *Saul-dah'-doh*

Solid. Sólido. *Sau'-le-doh*

Something. Algo. *Ahl'-goh*

Song. Canción. *Cahn-the-aun'*

Sore. Llaga; dolorido. *Lyah'-gah; dau-lau-ree'-doh*

Sound. Sonido; sano. *Saunee'-doh; sah'-noh*

Soup. Sopa. *Sau'-pah*

Sour. Ágrio. *Ah'-gre-oh*

Souvenir. Recuerdo. *Reh-cooer'-doh*

Space. Espacio. *Es-pah'-the-oh*

Sparking plug. Bujía. *Boohee'-ah*

Speak. Hablar. *Ah-blar'*

Special. Especial. *Es-peh-the-ahl'*

Speed. Velocidad. *Veh-lau-the-dahd'*

Spend. Gastar. *Gas-tar'*

Spider. Araña. *Ah-rah'-nyah*

Spring. Primavera; muelle. *Pre-mah-veh'-rah; moo-eh'-lyeh*

Squall. Borrasca. *Baur-ras'-cah*

Square. Plaza; cuadrado. *Plah'-thah; coo-ah-drah'-doh*

Squeal. Chillido. *Che-lyee'-doh*

Stage. Escenario. *Es-the-nah'-re-oh*

Stain. Mancha. *Mahn'-chah*

Stain remover. Quitamanchas. *Kee-tah-mahn'-chas*

Stairs. Escalera. *Es-cah-leh'-rah*

Stamp. Sello. *Seh'-lyoh*

Star. Estrella. *Es-treh'-lyah*

Starch. Almidón. *Ahl-medaun'*

Start. Comenzar. *Cau-menthar'*

Statue. Estatua. *Es-tah'-too-ah*

Steak. Filete. *Fe-leh'-teh*

Steam. Vapor. *Vah-paur'*

Steering-wheel. Volante. *Vaulahn'-teh*

Stick. Palo. *Pah'-lo*

Sticking plaster. Esparadrapo. *Es-pah-rah-drah'-poh*

Stiff. Tieso. *Te-eh'-soh*

Sting. Picadura. *Pe-cah-doo'-rah*

Stirrup. Estribo. *Es-tree'-boh*

Stone. Piedra. *Pe-eh'-drah*

Stop. Parada; detener. *Pahrah'-dah; deh-teh-ner'*

Storm. Tempestad. *Tem-pestahd'*

Strange. Extraño. *Ex-trah'-nyoh*

Stranger. Forastero. *Fau-rasteh'-roh*

Straw. Paja. *Pah'-hah*

Strawberry. Fresa. *Freh'-sah*

Stream. Arroyo. *Ar-rau'-yoh*

Strike. Golpe; huelga; golpear. *Gaul'-peh; oo-el'-gah; gaulpeh-ar'*

166

Student. Estudiante. *Es-too-de-ahn'-teh*

Study. Estudio; estudiar. *Es-too'-de-oh; es-too-de ar'*

Stupid. Necio. *Neh'-the-oh*

Subject. Asunto; súbdito. *Ah-soon'-toh; soob'-de-toh*

Success. Éxito. *Ek'-se-toh*

Suicide. Suicidio. *Soo-e-thee'-de-oh*

Suit. Traje. *Trah'-heh*

Sun. Sol. *Saul*

Sunrise. Amanecer. *Ah-mah-neh-ther'*

Supper. Cena. *Theh'-nah*

Surgical. Quirúrgico. *Ke-roor'-he-coh*

Swedish. Sueco. *Soo-eh'-coh*

Sweep. Barrer. *Bar-rer'*

Sweet. Dulce; caramelo. *Dool'-theh; cah-rah-meh'-loh*

Swim. Nadar. *Nah-dar'*

Swindle. Estafa. *Ehs-tah'-fah*

Swiss. Suizo. *Soo-ee'-thoh*

Switch. Interruptor. *In-ter-roop-taur'*

Sword. Espada. *Es-pah'-dah*

Sympathy. Simpatía. *Sim-pah-tee'-ah*

Tablecloth. Mantel. *Mahn-tel'*

Tail. Cola. *Cau'-lah*

Tailor. Sastre. *Sas'-treh*

Take. Tomar. *Tau-mar'*

Take off. Despegar. *Des-peh-gar'*

Tanned. Bronceado. *Braun-the-ah'-doh*

Taste. Gusto; probar; saborear. *Goos'-toh; prau-bar'; sah-bau-reh-ar'*

Tavern. Taberna. *Tah-ber'-nah*

Tea-pot. Tetera. *Teh-teh'-rah*

Teach. Enseñar. *En-seh-nyar'*

Teacher. Maestro; profesor. *Mah-es'-troh; pro-feh-sor'*

Teeth. Dentadura. *Den-tah-doo'-rah*

Telegram. Telegrama. *Teh-leh-grah'-mah*

Tell. Narrar; contar. *Nar-rar'; caun-tar'*

Temperature. Fiebre. *Fe-eh'-breh*

Tenant. Inquilino. *In-ke-lee'-noh*

Thank. Agradecer. *Ah-grah-deh-ther'*

Theft. Robo. *Rau'-boh*

Therapeutics. Terapéutica. *The-rah-peh'-oo-te-cah*

Thermometer. Termómetro. *Ter-mau'-meh-troh*

Thick. Espeso. *Es-peh'-soh*

Thief. Ladrón. *Lah-draun'*

Thin. Delgado. *Del-gah'-doh*

Thing. Cosa. *Cau'-sah*

Think. Pensar. *Pen-sar'*

Thread. Hilo. *Ee'-loh*

Throat. Garganta. *Gar-gahn'-tah*

Throw. Tirar. *Te-rar'*

Ticket inspector. Revisor. *Reh-ve-saur'*

Tide. Marea. *Mah-reh'-ah*

Tie. Corbata. *Caur-bah'-tah*

Time. Tiempo. *Te-em'-poh*

Timid. Tímido. *Tee'-me-doh*

Toast. Tostada; brindis. *Taus-tah'-dah; breen'-dis*

Tobacco. Tabaco. *Tah-bah'-coh*

Toe. Dedo del pie. *Deh'-doh del pe-eh'*

Toilet-case. Neceser. *Neh-theh-ser'*

167

Toll. Peaje. *Peh-ah'-heh*

Tongue. Lengua. *Len'-goo-ah*

Too much. Demasiado. *Deh-mah-se-ah'-doh*

Tooth. Diente; muela. *De-en'-teh; moo-eh'-lah*

Top. Cima. *Thee'-mah*

Topographer. Topógrafo. *Tau-pau'-grah-foh*

Torch. Linterna. *Lin-ter'-nah*

Touch. Tacto; tocar. *Tac'-toh; tau-car'*

Tow. Remolcar. *Reh-maul-car'*

Towel. Toalla. *Tau-ah'-lyah*

Track. Pista; ruta. *Pees'-tah; roo'-tah*

Transfer. Transferir. *Trans-feh-reer'*

Transfusion. Transfusión. *Trans-foo-se-aun'*

Translate. Traducir. *Trah-doo-theer'*

Trapezium. Trapecio. *Trah-peh'-the-oh*

Tree. Árbol. *Ar'-baul*

Trick. Engaño. *En-gah'-nyoh*

Trolleybus. Trolebús. *Trau-leh-boos'*

Tropical. Tropical. *Trau-pe-cahl'*

Trousers. Pantalones. *Pahn-tah-lau'-nes*

Truck. Camión. *Cah-me-aun'*

Truly. Verdaderamente. *Ver-dah-deh-rah-men'-teh*

Trunk. Baúl. *Bah-ool'*

Truth. Verdad. *Ver-dahd'*

Try. Tratar; intentar. *Trah-tar'; in-ten-tar'*

Tunnel. Túnel. *Too'-nel*

Turkish. Turco. *Toor'-coh*

Type. Tipo. *Tee'-poh*

Typist. Mecanógrafo. *Meh-cah-nau'-grah-foh*

Ulcer. Úlcera. *Ool'-theh-rah*

Umbrella. Paraguas. *Pah-rah'-goo-as*

Uncomfortable. Incómodo. *In-cau'-mau-doh*

Underground. Subterráneo. *Soob-ter-rah'-neh-oh*

Understand. Comprender. *Caum-pren-der'*

Undress. Desvestir. *Des-ves-teer'*

Unemployed. Desocupado. *Des-au-coo-pah'-doh*

Uneven. Desigual. *Des-e-goo-ahl'*

Unfair. Injusto. *In-hoos'-toh*

Unfasten. Soltar; desatar. *Saul-tar'; des-ah-tar'*

Unfortunate. Desafortunado. *Des-ah-faur-too-nah'-doh*

Unpack. Desempaquetar. *Des-em-pah-keh-tar'*

Unpleasant. Desagradable. *Des-ah-grah-dah'-bleh*

Unusual. Raro. *Rah'-roh*

Urbanization. Urbanización. *Oor-bah-ne-thah-the-aun'*

Use. Uso; usar. *Oo'-soh; oo-sar'*

Used to. Acostumbrado. *Ah-caus-toom-brah'-doh*

Useful. Útil. *Oo'-tel*

Useless. Inútil. *In-oo'-teel*

Usher. Ujier; acomodador. *Oo-her-er'; ah-cau-mau-dah-daur'*

Vacation. Vacación. *Vah-cah-the-aun'*

Vaccinate. Vacunar. *Vah-coo-nar'*

Valise. Maleta. *Mah-leh'-tah*

168

Valuable. Valioso. *Vah-le-au'-soh*

Valve. Válvula. *Vahl'-voo-lah*

Velvet. Terciopelo. *Ter-the-au-peh'-loh*

Vest. Chaleco. *Chah-leh'-coh*

Village. Aldea. *Ahl-deh'-ah*

Vinegar. Vinagre. *Ve-nah'-greh*

Visa. Visado. *Ve-sah'-doh*

Visit. Visita. *Ve-see'-tah*

Voice. Voz. *Vauth*

Voltage. Voltaje. *Vaul-tah'-heh*

Vomit. Vomitar. *Vau-me-tar'*

Wait. Esperar. *Es-peh-rar'*

Waiting-room. Sala de espera. *Sah'-lah deh es-peh'-rah*

Walk. Andar. *Ahn-dar'*

Wall. Pared. *Pah-red'*

Wallet. Cartera. *Car-teh'-rah*

Walnut. Nuez; nogal. *Noo-eth'; nau-gahl'*

Wash. Lavar. *Lah-var'*

Wave. Ola; onda. *Au'-lah; aun'-dah*

Weak. Débil. *Deh'-beel*

Week. Semana. *Seh-mah'-nah*

Well-mannered. Educado. *Eh-doo-cah'-doh*

West. Oeste. *Au-es'-teh*

Wet. Húmedo; mojado. *Oo'-meh-doh; mau-hah'-doh*

Whale. Ballena. *Bah-lyeh'-nah*

Wheel. Rueda. *Roo-eh'-dah*

Whimper. Lloriqueo. *Lyau-re-keh'-oh*

Wide. Ancho. *Ahn'-choh*

Widow. Viuda. *Ve-oo'-dah*

Wild. Salvaje. *Sahl-vah'-heh*

Willing. Dispuesto. *Dis-poo-es'-toh*

Window. Ventana. *Ven-tah'-nah*

Wire. Alambre. *Ah-lahm'-breh*

Wise. Sabio. *Sah'-be-oh*

Wish. Deseo; desear. *Deh-seh'-oh; deh-seh-ar'*

With. Con. *Caun*

Wolf. Lobo. *Lau'-boh*

Woman. Mujer. *Moo-her'*

Wood. Madera. *Mah-deh'-rah*

Wool. Lana. *Lah'-nah*

Word. Palabra. *Pah-lah'-brah*

Work. Trabajo; trabajar. *Trah-bah'-hoh; trah-bah-har'*

Workman. Jornalero; trabajador. *Jor-nah-leh'-roh; trah-bah-hah-daur'*

World. Mundo. *Moon'-doh*

Worn out. Usado; gastado. *Oo-sah'-doh; gas-tah'-doh*

Wound. Herida. *Eh-ree'-dah*

Wrap. Envolver. *En-vaul-ver'*

Wrath. Ira. *Ee'-rah*

Write. Escribir. *Es-cree-beer'*

Wrong. Equivocado; injusto. *Eh-ke-vau-cah'-doh; in-hoos'-toh*

X-Rays. Rayos X. *Rah'-yohs eh'-kis*

Yacht. Yate. *Yah'-teh*

Yard. Patio; yarda. *Pah'-te-oh; yar'-dah*

Yellow. Amarillo. *Ah-mah-ree'-lyoh*

Young. Joven. *Hau'-ven*

Zoo. Zoológico. *Thau-au-lau'-he-coh*

169

SPANISH-ENGLISH DICTIONARY

Abajo. *Ah-bah'-hoh.* Down

Abanico. *Ah-bah-nee'-coh.* Fan

Abierto. *Ah-be-er'-toh.* Open

Abogado. *Ah-bau-gah'-doh.* Lawyer

Abrelatas. *Ah-breh-lah'-tas.* Can opener (Tin opener)

Abrigo. *Ah-bree'-goh.* Coat

Abrir. *Ah-breer'.* Open

Absolutamente. *Ab-sau-loo-tah-men'-te.* Absolutely

Absoluto. *Ab-sau-loo'-toh.* Absolute

Acabar. *Ah-cah-bar'.* Finish

Academia. *Ah-cah-deh'-me-ah.* Academy

Acampar. *Ah-cahm-par'.* Camp

Accidente. *Ac-se-dehn'-teh.* Accident

Aceite. *Ah-thei'-teh.* Oil

Aceituna. *Ah-thei-too'-nah.* Olive

Acento. *Ah-then'-toh.* Accent

Aceptar. *Ah-thep-tar'.* Accept

Acera. *Ah-theh'-rah.* Pavement (Sidewalk)

Acomodador. *Ah-cau-mau-dah-daur'.* Usher

Acompañar. *Ah-caum-pah-nyar'.* Accompany

Acostarse. *Ah-caus-tar'-seh.* Go to bed

Acostumbrado. *Ah-caus-toom-brah'-doh.* Used to

Activo. *Ac-tee'-voh.* Active

Actor. *Ac-taur'.* Actor

Adjetivo. *Ad-heh-tee'-voh.* Adjective

Admiración. *Ad-me-rah-the-aun'.* Admiration

Admitir. *Ad-me-teer'.* Admit

Adorable. *Ah-dau-rah'-bleh.* Adorable

Aduanero. *Ah-doo-ah-neh'-roh.* Customs officer

Afectuoso. *Ah-fec-too-au'-soh.* Affectionate

Afeitar. *Ah-fei-tar'.* Shave

Aficionado. *Ah-fe-the-au-nah'-doh.* Fan

Afortunadamente. *Ah-faur-too-nah-dah-men'-teh.* Fortunately

Agente. *Ah-hen'-teh.* Agent

Agradable. *Ah-grah-dah'-ble.* Pleasant

Agradecer. *Ah-gra-deh-ther'.* Thank

Agrio. *Ah'-gre-oh.* Sour

Agua. *Ah'-goo-ah.* Water

Agudo. *Ah-goo'-doh.* Sharp

Aguja. *Ah-goo'-hah.* Needle

Agujero. *Ah-goo-heh'-roh.* Hole

Ahogarse. *Ah-au-gar'-seh.* Get drowned

Ahora. *Ah-au'-rah.* Now

Aire. *Ah'-e-reh.* Air

Ajo. *Ah'-hoh.* Garlic

Alambre. *Ah-lahm'-breh.* Wire

Alarma. *Ah-lar'-mah.* Alarm

Alcalde. *Ah-cahl'-deh.* Mayor

Alcanzar. *Ahl-cahn-thar'.* Reach

Alcoba. *Ahl-cau'-bah.* Bedroom

Alcohol. *Ahl-cau-aul'.* Alcohol

Aldea. *Ahl-deh'-ah.* Village

Alegre. *Ah-leh'-greh.* Gay

Alfabeto. *Ahl-fah-beh'-toh.* Alphabet

Alfiler. *Ahl-fe-ler'.* Pin

Alfombra. *Ahl-faum'-brah.* Rug. Carpet

Algo. *Ahl'-goh.* Something. Anything

Algodón. *Ahl-gau-daun'.* Cotton

Alimento. *Ah-le-men'-toh.* Food

Almendra. *Ahl-men'-drah.* Almond

Almidón. *Ahl-me-daun'.* Starch

Almirante. *Ahl-me-rahn'-teh.* Admiral

Almohada. *Ahl-mau-ah'-dah.* Pillow

Almorzar. *Ahl-maur-thar'.* Have lunch

Alojamiento. *Ah-lau-hah-me-en'-toh.* Lodging

Alquilar. *Ahl-ke-lar'.* Rent

Alrededor. *Ahl-reh-deh-daur'.* Around

Alto. *Ahl'-toh.* High. Tall

Alumno. *Ah-loom'-noh.* Student; pupil

Amable. *Ah-mah'-bleh.* Kind

Amanecer. *Ah-mah-neh-ther'.* Sunrise

Amar. *Ah-mar'.* Love

Amargo. *Ah-mar'-goh.* Bitter

Amarillo. *Ah-mah-ree'-lyoh.* Yellow

Ambos. *Ahm'-bohs.* Both

Ambulancia. *Ahm-boo-lahn'-the-ah.* Ambulance

Amigo. *Ah-mee'-goh.* Friend

Amor. *Ah-maur'.* Love

Amortiguador. *Ah-maur-te-goo-ah-daur'.* Shock absorber

Ancho. *Ahn'-choh.* Wide

Andar. *Ahn-dar'.* Walk

Ángel. *Ahn'-hel.* Angel

Anillo. *Ah-nee'-lyo.* Ring

Animal. *Ah-ne-mahl'.* Animal

Anoche. *Ah-nau'-cheh.* Last night

Anochecer. *Ah-nau-cheh-ther'.* Evening; get dark

Ansioso. *Ahn-se-au'-soh.* Anxious

Anterior. *Ahn-teh-re-aur'.* Former

Antes. *Ahn'-tehs.* Before

Antiguo. *Ahn-tee'-goo-oh.* Ancient

Anuncio. *Ah-noon'-the-oh.* Advertisement

Apellido. *Ah-peh-lyee'-doh.* Last name

Aplazar. *Ah-plah-thar'.* Postpone

Apreciar. *Ah-preh-the-ar'.* Appreciate

Aprender. *Ah-pren-der'.* Learn

Aproximadamente. *Ah-prauc-se-mah-dah-men'-teh.* Approximately

Araña. *Ah-rah'-nyah.* Spider

Árbitro. *Ar'-be-troh.* Referee

Árbol. *Ar'-baul.* Tree

Arco. *Ar'-coh.* Arch

Arena. *Ah-reh'-nah.* Sand

Armario. *Ar-mah'-re-oh.* Cupboard

Arquitecto. *Ar-ke-tec'-toh.* Architect

Arroyo. *Ar-rau'-yoh.* Stream

Artificial. *Ar-te-fe-the-ahl'.* Artificial

Artista. *Ar-tees'-tah.* Artist

Arzobispo. *Ar-thau-bees'-poh.* Archbishop

Asado. *Ah-sah'-doh.* Roast

Ascensor. *As-then-saur'.* Lift (Elevator)

Asegurar. *Ah-seh-goo-rar'.* Insure

Asesinar. *Ah-seh-se-nar'.* Murder

Asiento. *Ah-se-en'-toh.* Seat

Asistir. *Ah-sis-teer'.* Assist

Áspero. *As'-peh-roh.* Rough

Asunto. *Ah-soon'-toh.* Subject

Asustar. *Ah-soos-tar'.* Frighten

Aterrizar. *Ah-ter-re-thar'.* Land

Atraco. *Ah-trah'-coh.* Mugging

Ausente. *Ah-oo-sen'-teh.* Absent

Autoridad. *Ah-oo-tau-re-dahd'.* Authority

Avanzar. *Ah-vahn-thar'.* Advance

Avergonzado. *Ah-ver-gaun-thah'-doh.* Ashamed

Avería. *Ah-veh-ree'-ah.* Breakdown

Ayudar. *Ah-yoo-dar'.* Help

Babor. *Bah-baur'.* Port

Bahía. *Bah-ee'-ah.* Bay

Bailar. *Bah-e-lar'.* Dance

Baile. *Bah'-e-leh.* Dance

Bajar. *Bah-har'.* Come down; go down

Balanza. *Bah-lahn'-thah.* Scales

Balcón. *Bahl-caun'.* Balcony

Ballena. *Bah-lyeh'-nah.* Whale

Bañarse. *Bah-nyar'-seh.* Bathe

Baraja. *Bah-rah'-hah.* Pack of cards

Barba. *Bar'-bah.* Beard

Barrer. *Bar-rer'.* Sweep

Barrio. *Bar'-re-oh.* District

Basura. *Bah-soo'-rah.* Garbage

Batalla. *Bah-tah'-lyah.* Battle

Baúl. *Bah-ool'.* Trunk

Beber. *Beh-ber'.* Drink

Belleza. *Beh-lyeh'-thah.* Beauty

Beneficio. *Beh-neh-fe'-the-oh.* Profit

Beso. *Beh'-soh.* Kiss

Biblioteca. *Be-ble-au-teh'-cah.* Library

Bicicleta. *Be-the-cleh'-tah.* Bicycle

Bigote. *Be-gau'-teh.* Mustache

Bocina. *Bau-thee'-nah.* Horn

Bodega. *Bau-deh'-gah.* Cellar

Bolígrafo. *Bau-lee'-grah-foh.* Ball point pen

Bolsillo. *Baul-see'-lyoh.* Pocket

Bolso. *Baul'-soh.* Handbag

Bombilla. *Baum-bee'-lyah.* Bulb

Borrasca. *Baur-ras'-cah.* Squall

Botella. *Bau-teh'-lyah.* Bottle

Botiquín. *Bau-te-keen'.* First aid kit

Botón. *Bau-taun'.* Button

Bragas. *Brah'-gas.* Panties

Broma. *Brau'-mah.* Joke

Bronceado. *Braun-the-ah'-doh.* Tanned

Brújula. *Broo'-hoo-lah.* Compass

Bufanda. *Boo-fahn'-dah.* Scarf

Búho. *Boo'-oh.* Owl

Bujía. *Boo-hee'-ah.* Sparking plug

Burro. *Boor'-roh.* Donkey

Buscar. *Boos-car'.* Look for

Buzón. *Boo-thaun'.* Letter box

Caballero. *Cah-bah-lyeh'-roh.* Gentleman

Caballo. *Cah-bah'-lyoh.* Horse

Cabello. *Cah-beh'-lyoh.* Hair

Cabeza. *Cah-beh'-thah.* Head

Cable. *Cah'-bleh.* Cable

Cacahuete. *Cah-cah-oo-eh'-teh.* Peanut

Caer. *Cah-er'.* Fall

Caja. *Cah'-hah.* Box

Cajón. *Cah-haun'.* Drawer

Calendario. *Cah-len-dah'-re-oh.* Calendar

Calentar. *Cah-len-tar'.* Heat

Calidad. *Cah-le-dahd'.* Quality

Caliente. *Cah-le-en'-teh.* Hot

Calor. *Cah-laur'.* Heat

Cama. *Cah'-mah.* Bed

Camarote. *Cah-mah-rau'-teh.* Cabin

Cambiar. *Cahm-be-ar'.* Change

Cambio. *Cahm'-be-oh.* Change

Camino. *Cah-mee'-noh.* Road, way

Camión. *Cah-me-aun'.* Truck

Campana. *Cahm-pah'-nah.* Bell

Campesino. *Cahm-peh-see'-noh.* Peasant

Canal. *Cah-nahl'.* Canal

Canción. *Cahn-the-aun'.* Song

Cangrejo. *Cahn-greh'-hoh.* Crab

Cantar. *Cahn-tar'.* Sing

Cantidad. *Cahn-te-dahd'.* Quantity

Capilla. *Cah-pee'-lyah.* Chapel

Cara. *Cah'-rah.* Face

Caracol. *Cah-rah-caul'.* Snail

Caramelo. *Cah-rah-meh'-loh.* Sweet

Carbón. *Car-baun'.* Coal

Cárcel. *Car'-thel.* Jail

Carga. *Car'-gah.* Freight, load

Carta. *Car'-tah.* Letter

Cartera. *Car-teh'-rah.* Wallet

Cartero. *Car-teh'-roh.* Postman

Casa. *Cah'-sah.* House

Casado. *Cah-sah'-doh.* Married

Castigar. *Cas-te-gar'.* Punish

Castillo. *Cas-tee'-lyoh.* Castle

Catálogo. *Cah-tah'-lau-goh.* Catalogue

Catarro. *Cah-tar'-roh.* Cold

Católico. *Cah-tau'-le-coh.* Catholic

Caucho. *Cah'-oo-choh.* Rubber

Caza. *Cah'-tha.* Hunting

Cebolla. *Theh-bau'-lyah.* Onion

Cementerio. *Theh-men-teh'-re-oh.* Cemetery

Cena. *Theh'-nah.* Supper. Dinner

Cenicero. *The-ne-theh'-roh.* Ashtray

Cepillar. *Theh-pe-lyar'.* Brush

Cerdo. *Ther'-doh.* Pig

Cerebro. *Theh-reh'-broh.* Brain

Cerilla. *Theh-ree'-lyah.* Match

Cerradura. *Ther-rah-doo'-rah.* Lock

Ciego. *The-eh'-goh.* Blind

Cielo. *The-eh'-loh.* Sky; heaven

Ciencia. *The-en'-the-ah.* Science

173

Científico. *The-en-tee'-fe-coh.* Scientific

Cierto. *The-er'-toh.* Certain

Cima. *Thee'-mah.* Top

Cinta adhesiva. *Theen'-tah ah-deh-see'-vah.* Adhesive tape

Cinturón. *Thin-too-raun'.* Belt

Círculo. *Theer'-coo-loh.* Circle

Cita. *Thee'-tah.* Appointment

Cola. *Cau'-lah.* Tail

Colchón. *Caul-chaun'.* Mattress

Colegio. *Cau-leh'-he-oh.* School; college

Comedor. *Cau-meh-daur'.* Dinning-room

Comenzar. *Cau-men-thar'.* Start

Comerciante. *Cau-mer-the-ahn'-teh.* Businessman

Cómico. *Cau'-me-coh.* Funny

Comida. *Cau-mee'-dah.* Food; meal; dinner

Comisaría. *Cau-me-sah-ree'-ah.* Police Station

Comodidad. *Cau-mau-de-dahd'.* Comfort

Compañía. *Caum-pah-nyee'-ah.* Company

Comparación. *Caum-pah-rah-the-aun'.* Comparison

Componer. *Caum-pau-ner'.* Repair

Comprar. *Caum-prar'.* Buy

Comprender. *Caum-pren-der'.* Understand

Común. *Cau-moon'.* Common

Comunista. *Cau-moo-nees'-tah.* Communist

Condición. *Caun-de-the-aun'.* Condition

Conducir. *Caun-doo-theer'.* Drive

Conejo. *Cau-neh'-hoh.* Rabbit

Conferencia. *Caun-feh-ren'-the-ah.* Lecture

Confuso. *Caun-foo'-soh.* Confused

Congelado. *Caun-heh-lah'-doh.* Frozen

Congreso. *Caun-greh'-soh.* Congress

Conmigo. *Caun-mee'-goh.* With me

Conocer. *Cau-nau-ther'.* Know

Conseguir. *Caun-seh-gheer'.* Get

Consejo. *Caun-seh'-hoh.* Advice

Considerar. *Caun-se-deh-rar'.* Consider

Consigna. *Caun-seeg'-nah.* Left luggage office

Consonante. *Caun-sau-nahn'-teh.* Consonant

Constipado. *Cauns-te-pah'-doh.* Cold

Construir. *Cauns-troo-eer'.* Build

Cónsul. *Caun'-sool.* Consul

Contagioso. *Caun-tah-he-au'-soh.* Infectious

Contar. *Caun-tar'.* Count

Contener. *Caun-teh-ner'.* Contain

Contento. *Caun-ten'-toh.* Content

Contestación. *Caun-tes-tah-the-aun'.* Answer; reply

Continuar. *Caun-te-noo-ar'.* Continue

Conversación. *Caun-ver-sah-the-aun'.* Conversation

Copa. *Cau'-pah.* Glass

Copia. *Cau'-pe-ah.* Copy

Corazón. *Cau-rah-thaun'.* Heart

Corbata. *Caur-bah'-tah.* Tie

Corcho. *Caur'-choh.* Cork

Cortar. *Caur-tar'.* Cut

Cosa. *Cau'-sah.* Thing

Coser. *Cau-ser'.* Sew

Costa. *Caus'-tah.* Coast

Costilla. *Caus-tee'-lyah.* Rib

Costumbre. *Caus-toom'-breh.* Custom

Creer. *Creh-er'.* Believe

Criada. *Cre-ah'-dah.* Maid

Cristiano. *Cris-te-ah'-noh.* Christian

Cruz. *Crooth.* Cross

Cruz Roja. *Crooth Rau'-hah.* Red Cross

Cruzar. *Croo-thar'.* Cross

Cuaderno. *Coo-ah-der'-noh.* Notebook

Cuadro. *Coo-ah'-droh.* Picture

Cucaracha. *Coo-cah-rah'-chah.* Cockroach

Cuchillo. *Coo-chee'-lyoh.* Knife

Cuerda. *Coo-er'-dah.* Rope

Cuero. *Coo-eh'-roh.* Leather

Culebra. *Coo-leh'-brah.* Snake

Culpa. *Cool'-pah.* Fault

Cumpleaños. *Coom-pleh-ah'-nyohs.* Birthday

Cura. *Coo'-ra.* Priest

Chaleco. *Chah-leh'-coh.* Vest

Champaña. *Chahm-pah'-nyah.* Champagne

Champú. *Chahm-poo'.* Shampoo

Chaqueta. *Chah-keh'-tah.* Jacket

Chicle. *Chee'-cleh.* Chewing-gum

Chillido. *Che-lyee'-doh.* Squeal

Chocolate. *Chau-cau-lah'-teh.* Chocolate

Choque. *Chau'-keh.* Collision

Dama. *Dah'-mah.* Lady

Daño. *Dah'-nyoh.* Damage

Dar. *Dar.* Give

Deber. *Deh-ber'.* Must

Debidamente. *Deh-be-dah-men'-teh.* Properly

Débil. *Deh'-beel.* Weak

Decidir. *Deh-the-deer'.* Decide

Decir. *Deh-theer'.* Tell; say

Declarar. *Deh-clah-rar'.* Declare

Dedo de la mano. *Deh' doh deh lah mah'-noh.* Finger

Dedo del pie. *Deh'-doh del pe-eh'.* Toe

Dejar. *Deh-har'.* Leave

Delgado. *Del-gah'-doh.* Thin

Demasiado. *Deh-mah-se-ah'-doh.* Too much

Democracia. *Deh-mau-crah'-the-ah.* Democracy

Dentadura. *Den-tah-doo'-rah.* Teeth

Dentro. *Den'-troh.* Inside

Denunciar. *Deh-noon-thee-ahr'.* Report

Dependiente. *Deh-pen-de-en'-teh.* Shop assistant

Depósito. *Deh-pau'-se-toh.* Deposit

Derechos. *Deh-reh'-chohs.* Rights

Desafortunado. *Des-ah-faur-too-nah'-doh.* Unfortunate

Desagradable. *Des-ah-grah-dah'-bleh.* Unpleasant

175

Desagüe. *Des-ah'-goo-eh.* Drainage

Desarrollar. *Des-ar-rau-lyar'.* Develop

Descansar. *Des-cahn-sar'.* Rest

Descanso. *Des-cahn'-soh.* Rest

Descompuesto. *Des-caum-poo-es'-toh.* Out of order

Describir. *Des-cre-beer'.* Describe

Descuento. *Des-coo-en'-toh.* Discount

Desear. *Deh-seh-ar'.* Wish

Desempaquetar. *Des-em-pah-keh'tar'.* Unpack

Desengaño. *Des-en-gah'-nyoh.* Disappointment

Deseo. *Deh-seh'-oh.* Wish

Desgracia. *Des-grah'-the-ah.* Misfortune

Desierto. *Deh-se-er'-toh.* Desert

Desigual. *Des-e-goo-ahl'.* Uneven

Desmayarse. *Des-mah-yar'-se.* Faint

Desmayo. *Des-mah'-yoh.* Fainting

Desnudo. *Des-noo'-doh.* Naked

Desocupado. *Des-au-coo-pah'-doh.* Unemployed

Despacio. *Des-pah'-the-oh.* Slowly

Despedir. *Des-peh-deer'.* Dismiss

Despegar. *Des-peh-gar'.* Take off

Despertador. *Des-per-tah-daur'.* Alarm clock

Despierto. *Des-pe-er'-toh.* Awake

Desprender. *Des-pren-der'.* Unfasten

Desvestirse. *Des-ves-teer'-seh.* Undress

Detalle. *Deh-tah'-lyeh.* Detail

Detenerse. *Deh-teh-ner'-seh.* Stop

Deuda. *Deh'-oo-dah.* Debt

Diablo. *De-ah'-bloh.* Devil

Diamante. *De-ah-mahn'-teh.* Diamond

Diario. *De-ah'-re-oh.* Newspaper

Diarrea. *De-ar-reh'-ah.* Diarrhoea

Dibujar. *De-boo-har'.* Draw

Diccionario. *Dic-the-au-nah'-re-oh.* Dictionary

Dichoso. *De-chau'-soh.* Happy

Diente. *De-en'-teh.* Tooth

Diferencia. *De-feh-ren'-the-ah.* Difference

Difícil. *De-fee'-theel.* Difficult

Dimensión. *De-men-se-aun'.* Dimension

Dinero. *De-neh'-roh.* Money

Dios. *De-aus'.* God

Director. *De-rec-taur'.* Director

Dirigir. *De-re-heer'.* Direct

Disco. *Dees'-coh.* Record

Disculpa. *Dis-cool'-pah.* Excuse

Disgustar. *Dis-goos-tar'.* Displease

Disparate. *Dis-pah-rah'-teh.* Nonsense

Disparo. *Dis-pah'-roh.* Shot

Dispensar. *Dis-pen-sar'.* Excuse

Disponible. *Dis-pau-nee'-bleh.* Available

Dispuesto. *Dis-poo-es'-toh.* Willing

Disputar. *Dis-poo-tar'*. Argue

Distinto. *Dis-teen'-toh*. Different

Distraído. *Dis-trah-ee'-doh*. Absent-minded

Distribución. *Dis-tre-boo-the-aun'*. Distribution

Distrito. *Dis-tree'-toh*. District

Diversión. *De-ver-se-aun'*. Amusement

Divertirse. *De-ver teer'-seh*. Enjoy oneself

Dividir. *De-ve-deer'*. Divide

Divorcio. *De-vaur'-the-oh*. Divorce

Doble. *Dau'-bleh*. Double

Doctor. *Dauc-taur'*. Doctor

Documento. *Dau-coo-men'-toh*. Document

Dolor. *Dau-laur'*. Ache; pain

Domicilio. *Dau-me-the'-le-oh*. Home

Dormir. *Daur-meer'*. Sleep

Dormitorio. *Daur-me-tau'-re-oh*. Bedroom

Dosis. *Dau'-sis*. Dose

Ducha. *Doo'-chah*. Shower

Duende. *Doo-en'-deh*. Ghost

Dueño. *Doo-eh'-nyoh*. Owner

Dulce. *Dool'-theh*. Sweet

Duro. *Doo'-roh*. Hard

Echar. *Eh-c^har'*. Throw

Edad. *Eh-dahd'*. Age

Edificar. *Eh-de-fe-car'*. Build

Edificio. *Eh-de-fee'-the-oh*. Building

Educación. *Eh-doo-cah'-the-aun'*. Education

Educado. *Eh-doo-cah'-doh*. Well-mannered

Efecto. *Eh-fec'-toh*. Effect

Ejemplo. *Eh-hem'-ploh*. Example

Ejercicio. *Eh-her-thee'-the-oh*. Exercise

Ejército. *Eh-her'-the-toh*. Army

Elástico. *Eh-las'-te-coh*. Elastic

Elección. *Eh-lec-the-aun'*. Choice

Electricidad. *Eh-lec-tre-the-dahd'*. Electricity

Elefante. *Eh-leh-fahn'-teh*. Elephant

Elegir. *Eh-leh-heer'*. Choose

Embajada. *Ehm-bah-hah'-dah*. Embassy

Embalaje. *Em-bah-lah'-heh*. Packing

Embarcarse. *Em-bar-car'-seh*. Embark

Emoción. *Eh-mau-the-aun'*. Emotion

Empalme. *Em-pahl'-meh*. Coupling

Emperador. *Em-peh-rah-daur'*. Emperor

Empezar. *Em-peh-thar'*. Begin; start

Empleado. *Em-pleh-ah'-doh*. Employee

Empleo. *Em-pleh'-oh*. Job

Empujar. *Em-poo-har'*. Push

Enaguas. *Eh-nah'-goo-as*. Petticoat

Encaje. *En-cah'-heh*. Lace

Encargado. *En-car-gah'-doh*. Attendant

Encendedor. *En-then-deh-daur'*. Lighter

Encender. *En-then-der'*. Light

Encontrar. *En-caun-trar'*. Meet; find

Encuentro. *En-coo-en'-troh.* Meeting

Enemigo. *Eh-neh-mee'-goh.* Enemy

Energía. *Eh-ner-hee'-ah.* Energy

Enfermedad. *En-fer-meh-dahd'.* Sickness

Enfermera. *En-fer-meh'-rah.* Nurse

Enfermo. *En-fer'-moh.* Ill; sick

Engañar. *En-gah-nyar'.* Deceive

Engaño. *En-gah'-nyoh.* Trick

Engordar. *En-gaur-dar'.* Get fat

Engrasar. *En-grah-sar'.* Grease

Enojado. *Eh-nau-hah'doh.* Angry

Enseñar. *En-seh-nyar'.* Teach

Entender. *En-ten-der'.* Understand

Enteramente. *En-teh-rah-men'-teh.* Entirely

Entierro. *En-te-er'-roh.* Funeral

Entreacto. *En-treh-ahc'-toh.* Interval

Entregar. *En-treh-gar'.* Deliver

Entrevista. *En-treh-vees'-tah.* Interview

Enviar. *En-ve-ar'.* Send

Envolver. *En-vaul-ver'.* Wrap

Equipo. *Eh-kee'-poh.* Equipment

Equivocado. *Eh-ke-vau-cah'-doh.* Wrong

Equivocar. *Eh-ke-vau-car'.* Mistake

Error. *Er-raur'.* Error

Escalera. *Es-cah-leh'-rah.* Stairs

Escaparate. *Es-cah-pah-rah'-teh.* Shop window

Escape. *Es-cah'-peh.* Leak

Escaso. *Es-cah'-soh.* Scarce

Escena. *Es-theh'-nah.* Stage

Escoba. *Es-cau'-bah.* Broom

Escocés. *Es-cau-thes'.* Scotch

Escoger. *Es-cau-her'.* Choose

Escollo. *Es-cau'-lyoh* Reef

Escribiente. *Es-cre-be-en'-teh.* Clerk

Escribir. *Es-cre-beer'.* Write

Escuchar. *Es-coo-char'.* Listen

Escuela. *Es-coo-eh'-lah.* School

Esmeralda. *Es-meh-rahl'-dah.* Emerald

Espacio. *Es-pah'-the-oh.* Space

Espada. *Es-pah'-dah.* Sword

Esparadrapo. *Es-pah-rah-drah'-poh.* Sticking plaster

Especial. *Es-peh-the-ahl'.* Special

Especialidad. *Es-peh-the-ah-le-dahd'.* Speciality

Espectáculo. *Es-pec-tah'-coo-loh.* Show

Espejo. *Es-peh'-hoh.* Mirror

Esperanza. *Es-peh-rahn'-thah.* Hope

Esperar. *Es-peh-rar'.* Wait

Espeso. *Es-peh'-soh.* Thick

Espina. *Es-pee'-nah.* Fish bone

Esquina. *Es-kee'-nah.* Corner

Estafa. *Ehs-tah'-fah.* Swindle

Estatua. *Es-tah'-too-ah.* Statue

Estrecho. *Es-treh'-choh.* Narrow

Estrella. *Es-treh'-lyah.* Star

Estreñimiento. *Es-treh-nye-me-en'-toh.* Constipation

Estribo. *Es-tree'-boh.* Stirrup

Estropear. *Es-trau-peh-ar'.* Damage

Estudiante. *Es too-de-ahn'-teh.* Student

Estudiar. *Es-too-de-ar'.* Study

Etiqueta. *Eh-te keh'-tah.* Label

Evidente. *Eh-ve den'-teh.* Obvious

Evitar. *Eh-ve-tar'.* Avoid

Exacto. *Ek-sahc'-toh.* Exact

Examen. *Ek-sah'-men.* Examination

Excelente. *Ex-theh-len'-teh.* Excellent

Excepto. *Ex-thep'-toh.* Except

Excursión. *Ex-coor-se-aun'.* Excursion

Excusa. *Ex-coo'-sah.* Excuse

Éxito. *Ek'-se-toh.* Success

Explicar. *Ex-ple-car'.* Explain

Exportar. *Ex-paur-tar'.* Export

Exposición. *Ex-pau-se-the-aun'.* Exhibition

Expreso. *Ex-preh'-soh.* Express

Extranjero. *Ex-trahn-heh'-roh.* Foreigner

Extraño. *Ex-trah'-nyoh.* Strange

Fábrica. *Fah'-bre-cah.* Factory

Fácil. *Fah'-theel.* Easy

Falso. *Fahl'-soh.* False

Familia. *Fah-mee'-le-ah.* Family

Fango. *Fahn'-goh.* Mud

Fantasma. *Fahn-tas'-mah.* Ghost

Farmacia. *Far-mah'-the-ah.* Drugstore; chemist's

Faro. *Fah'-roh.* Beacon

Fiebre. *Fe-eh'-breh.* Temperature

Fiesta. *Fe-es'-tah.* Party

Fijo. *Fee'-hoh.* Fixed

Filete. *Fe-leh'-teh.* Steak

Fin. *Feen.* End

Firmar. *Feer-mar'.* Sign

Flojo. *Flau'-hoh.* Loose

Flor. *Flaur.* Flower

Fondo. *Faun'-doh.* Bottom

Forastero. *Fau-ras-teh'-roh.* Stranger

Forma. *Faur' mah.* Form

Fórmula. *Faur'-moo-lah.* Formula

Frasco. *Fras'-coh.* Bottle

Frecuentemente. *Freh-coo-en-teh-men'-teh.* Frequently

Fréjol. *Freh'-haul.* Bean

Freno. *Freh'-noh.* Brake

Fresa. *Freh'-sah.* Strawberry

Frío. *Free'-oh.* Cold

Frito. *Free'-toh.* Fried

Frontera. *Fraun-teh'-rah.* Border

Fruta. *Froo'-tah.* Fruit

Fuego. *Foo-eh'-goh.* Fire

Fuente. *Foo-en'-teh.* Fountain

Fuerte. *Foo-er'-teh.* Strong

Fuerza. *Foo-er'-thah.* Power

Función. *Foon-the-aun'.* Performance

Fusil. *Foo-seel'.* Gun

Futuro. *Foo-too'-roh.* Future

Gabán. *Gah-bahn'.* Overcoat

Gabardina. *Gah-bar-dee'-nah.* Raincoat

Gafas. *Gah'-fas.* Glasses

Gala. *Gah'-lah.* Gala

Galaxia. *Gah-lac'-se-ah.* Galaxy

Galería. *Gah-leh-ree'-ah.* Gallery

Galón (measure). *Gah-laun'.* Gallon

Galleta. *Gah-lyeh'-tah.* Biscuit

Gallina. *Gah-lyee'-nah.* Hen

Gamba. *Gahm'-bah.* Prawn

Ganado. *Gah-nah'-doh.* Cattle

Garantizado. *Gah-rahn-te-thah'-do.* Guaranteed

Garganta. *Gar-gahn'-tah.* Throat

Gas. *Gas.* Gas

Gastar. *Gas-tar'.* Spend

Gastos. *Gas'-tohs.* Expenses

Gato. *Gah'-toh.* Cat

Generoso. *Heh-neh-rau'-soh.* Generous

Gente. *Hen'-teh.* People

Geografía. *Heh-au-grah-fee'-ah.* Geography

Gerente. *Heh-ren'-teh.* Manager

Ginebra. *Hee-neh'-brah.* Gin

Gobierno. *Gau-be-er'-noh.* Government

Golpe. *Gaul'-peh.* Blow

Gordo. *Gaur'-doh.* Fat

Gorra. *Gaur'-rah.* Cap

Gota. *Gau'-tah.* Drop

Grapa. *Grah'-pah.* Clamp

Grifo. *Gree'-foh.* Tap

Gripe. *Gree'-peh.* Influenza

Grito. *Gree'-toh.* Shout

Grosero. *Grau-seh'-roh.* Rude

Guapo. *Goo-ah'-poh.* Good-looking

Guardar. *Goo-ar-dar'.* Keep

Guijarro. *Ghe-har'-roh.* Pebble

Guisar. *Ghe-sar'.* Cook

Guitarra. *Ghe-tar'-rah.* Guitar

Gustar. *Goos-tar'.* Like

Haber. *Ah-ber'.* Have

Habitación. *Ah-be-tah-the-aun'.* Room

Habitante. *Ah-be-tahn'-teh.* Inhabitant

Hablar. *Ah-blar'.* Speak

Hacer. *Ah-ther'.* Make; do

Hambre. *Ahm'-breh.* Hunger

Haya. *Ah'-yah.* Beech-tree

Helado. *Eh-lah'-doh.* Ice-cream

Hembra. *Em'-brah.* Female

Herencia. *Eh-ren'-the-ah.* Heritage

Herida. *Eh-ree'-dah.* Wound; cut

Héroe. *Eh'-rau-eh.* Hero

Hervir. *Er-veer'.* Boil

Hielo. *E-eh'-loh.* Ice

Hierba. *E-er'-bah.* Grass

Hierro. *E-er'-roh.* Iron

Higo. *Ee'-goh.* Fig

Hilo. *Ee'-loh.* Thread

Hoja. *Au'-hah.* Leaf

Hombre. *Aum'-breh.* Man

Hombro. *Aum'-broh.* Shoulder

Homicida. *Au-me-thee'-dah.* Homicide

Homónimo. *Au-mau'-ne-moh.* Homonymous

Hondo. *Aun'-doh.* Deep

Hongo. *Aun'-goh.* Mushroom

Honor. *Au-naur'.* Honour

Honorario. *Au-nau-rah'-re-oh.* Honorary

Honrado. *Aun-rah'-doh.* Honest

Horizontal. *Au-re-thaun-tahl'.* Horizontal

Horno. *Aur'-noh.* Oven

Hospedaje. *Aus-peh-dah'-heh.* Lodging

Hospital. *Aus-pe-tahl'.* Hospital

Hospitalidad. *Aus-pe-tah-le-dahd'.* Hospitality

Huelga. *Oo-el'-gah.* Strike

Hueso. *Oo-eh'-soh.* Bone

Huida. *Oo-ee'-dah.* Flight

Hulla. *Oo'-lyah.* Pit-coal

Humano. *Oo-mah'-noh.* Human

Húmedo. *Oo'-meh-doh.* Wet

Humo. *Oo'-moh.* Smoke

Huracán. *Oo-rah-cahn'.* Hurricane

Idea. *E-deh'-ah.* Idea

Identificación. *E-den-te-fe-cah-the-aun'.* Identification

Idioma. *E-de-au'-mah.* Language

Idiota. *E-de-au'-tah.* Idiot

Iglesia. *E-gleh'-se-ah.* Church

Igual. *E-goo-ahl'.* Equal

Ilegal. *E-leh-gahl'.* Illegal

Ilustración. *E-loos-trah-the-aun'.* Illustration

Imaginación. *E-mah-he-nah-the-aun'.* Imagination

Imán. *E-mahn'.* Magnet

Imitación. *E-me-tah-the-aun'.* Imitation

Imperdible. *Im-per-dee'-bleh.* Safety-pin

Impermeable. *Im-per-meh-ah'-ble.* Raincoat

Incautar. *In-cah-oo-tar'.* Attach

Incidente. *In-the-den'-teh.* Incident

Incluido. *In-cloo-ee'-doh.* Included

Incoloro. *In-cau-lau'-roh.* Colourless

Incómodo. *In-cau'-mau-doh.* Uncomfortable

Incompleto. *In-caum-pleh'-toh.* Incomplete

Indemnización. *In-dem-ne-thah-the-aun'.* Indemnity

Independencia. *In-deh-pen-den'-the-ah.* Independence

Indicar. *In-de-car'.* Show

Indigestión. *In-de-hes-te-aun'.* Indigestion

Individuo. *In-de-vee'-doo-oh.* Individual

Infierno. *In-fe-er'-noh.* Hell

Injusto. *In-hoos'-toh.* Unfair

Inmigración. *In-me-grah-the-aun'.* Immigration

Inocente. *E-nau-then'-teh.* Innocent

Inquilino. *In-ke-lee'-noh.* Tenant

Insecto. *In-sec'-toh.* Insect

Insistir. *In-sis-teer'.* Insist

Inspeccionar. *Ins-pec-the-au-nar'.* Inspect

Intelectual. *In-teh-lec-too-ahl'.* Intellectual

Inteligente. *In-teh-le-hen'-teh.* Intelligent

Intenso. *In-ten'-soh.* Intense

Interpretar. *In-ter-preh-tar'.* Interpret

Interruptor. *In-ter-roop-taur'.* Switch

Inundación. *E-noon-dah-the-aun'.* Flood

Inútil. *In-oo'-teel.* Useless

Invalidez. *In-vah-le-deth'.* Disablement

Invasor. *In-vah-saur'.* Invader

Inventario. *In-ven-tah'-reh-oh.* Inventory

Investigar. *In-ves te-gar'.* Investigate

181

Inyección. *In-yec-the-aun'.* Injection

Ir. *Eer.* Go

Ira. *Ee'-rah.* Wrath

Iris. *Ee'-ris.* Iris

Ironía. *E-rau-nee'-ah.* Irony

Irritar. *Eer-re-tar'.* Irritate

Isla. *Ees'-lah.* Island

Izar. *E-thar'.* Hoist

Jabón. *Hah-baun'.* Soap

Jamón. *Hah-maun'.* Ham

Jardín. *Har-deen'.* Garden

Jerarquía. *Heh-rar-kee'-ah.* Hierarchy

Jerez. *Heh-reth'.* Sherry

Jornalero. *Haur-nah-leh'-roh.* Workman

Joven. *Hau'-ven.* Young

Joya. *Hau'-yah.* Jewel

Júbilo. *Hoo'-be-loh.* Joy

Juego. *Hoo-eh'-goh.* Game

Juez. *Hoo-eth'.* Judge

Jugar. *Hoo-gar'.* Play

Jugo. *Hoo'-goh.* Juice

Juicio. *Hoo-ee'-the-oh.* Judgement

Justicia. *Hoos-tee'-the-ah.* Justice

Justo. *Hoos'-toh.* Just

Juvenil. *Hoo-veh-neel'.* Youthful

Kilo. *Kee'-loh.* Kilogram

Kilociclo. *Ke-loh-thee'clo.* Kilocycle

Kilovatio. *Ke-loh-vah'-te-oh.* Kilowatt

Kimono. *Ke-mau'-noh.* Kimono

Kiosco. *Ke-aus'-coh.* Kiosk

Laberinto. *Lah-beh-reen'-toh.* Labyrinth

Labio. *Lah'-be-oh.* Lip

Labor. *Lah-baur'.* Labour

Lacre. *Lah'-creh.* Sealing wax

Ladrón. *Lah-draun'.* Thief

Lagarto. *Lah-gar'-toh.* Lizard

Lago. *Lah'-goh.* Lake

Lamentar. *Lah-men-tar'.* Regret

Lámpara. *Lahm'-pah-rah.* Lamp

Lana. *Lah'-nah.* Wool

Langosta. *Lahn-gaus'-tah.* Crayfish

Lápiz. *Lah'-pith.* Pencil

Latino. *La-tee'-noh.* Latin

Latinoamericano. *Lah-tee'-noh-ah-meh-re-cah'-noh.* Latin-American

Lavabo. *Lah-vah'-boh.* Hand basin

Lavandería. *Lah-vahn-deh-ree'-ah.* Laundry

Lavar. *Lah-var'.* Wash

Laxante. *Lac-sahn'-teh.* Laxative

Lección. *Lec-the-aun'.* Lesson

Leche. *Leh'-cheh.* Milk

Lechuga. *Leh-choo'-gah.* Lettuce

Leer. *Leh-er'.* Read

Lengua. *Lehn'-goo-ah.* Tongue

Lento. *Len'-toh.* Slow

Leña. *Leh'-nyah.* Wood

León. *Leh-aun'.* Lion

Letrero. *Leh-treh'-roh.* Sign

Levantarse. *Leh-vahn-tar'-seh.* Get up

Ley. *Leh'-e.* Law

Leyenda. *Leh-yen'-dah.* Legend

Libertad. *Le-ber-tahd'.* Liberty

Libra. *Lee'-brah.* Pound

Libre. *Lee'-breh.* Free

Libreta. *Le-bre'-tah.* Notebook

Libro. *Lee'-broh.* Book

Licencia. *Le-then'-the-ah.* Licence

Licor. *Le-caur'.* Liquor

Liga. *Lee'-gah.* Garter

Ligero. *Le-heh'-roh.* Light

Límite. *Lee'-me-teh.* Limit

Limón. *Le-maun'.* Lemon

Limonada. *Le-mau-nah'-dah.* Lemonade

Limpiar. *Lim-pe-ar'.* Clean

Lindo. *Leen'-doh.* Pretty

Lino. *Lee'-noh.* Linen

Linterna. *Lin-ter'-nah.* Torch

Liso. *Lee'-soh.* Smooth

Lista. *Lees'-tah.* List

Litera. *Le-teh'-rah.* Bunk

Lobo. *Lau'-boh.* Wolf

Loco. *Lau'-coh.* Crazy

Locomotora. *Lau-cau-mautau'-rah.* Locomotive

Locutor. *Lau-coo-taur'.* Announcer

Loma. *Lau'-mah.* Hill

Lugar. *Loo-gar'.* Place

Lujoso. *Loo-hau'-soh.* Luxurious

Lumbre. *Loom'-breh.* Fire

Luna. *Loo'-nah.* Moon

Luto. *Loo'-toh.* Mourning

Luz. *Looth.* Light

Llaga. *Lyah'-gah.* Sore

Llama. *Lyah'-mah.* Flame

Llamar. *Lyah-mar'.* Call

Llanura. *Lyah-noo'-rah.* Plain

Llave. *Lyah'-veh.* Key

Llegada. *Lyeh-gah'-dah.* Arrival

Llenar. *Lyeh-nar'.* Fill

Llorar. *Lyau-rar'.* Cry

Lloriqueo. *Lyau-re-keh'-oh.* Whimper

Llover. *Lyau-ver'.* Rain

Lluvia. *Lyoo've-ah.* Rain

Madeja. *Mah-deh'-hah.* Hank

Madera. *Mah-deh'-rah.* Wood

Madrugar. *Mah-droo-gar'.* Get up early

Maestro. *Mah-es'-troh.* Teacher

Magnífico. *Mag-nee'-fe-coh.* Magnificent

Maíz. *Mah-eeth'.* Corn

Mal. *Mahl.* Badly

Maleta. *Mah-leh'-tah.* Valise

Maletín. *Mah-leh-teen'.* Bag

Mancha. *Mahn'-chah.* Stain

Mandar. *Mahn-dar'.* Command

Manga. *Mahn'-gah.* Sleeve

Manivela. *Mah-ne-veh'-lah.* Handle

Mantel. *Mahn-tel'.* Tablecloth

Mantequilla. *Mahn-teh-kee'-lyah.* Butter

Mar. *Mar.* Sea

Marca. *Mar'-cah.* Mark

Marchar. *Mar-char'.* Go away

Marea. *Mah-reh'-ah.* Tide

Mármol. *Mar'-maul.* Marble

Marqués. *Mar-kes'.* Marquis

Martillo. *Mar-tee'-lyoh.* Hammer

Matar. *Mah-tar'.* Kill

Material. *Mah-teh-re-ahl'.* Material

Matrícula. *Ma-tree'-coo-lah.* Registration number

Mausoleo. *Mah-oo-sau-leh'-oh.* Mausoleum

183

Mayoría. *Mah-yau-ree'-ah.* Majority

Mecanógrafo. *Meh-cah-nau'-grah-foh.* Typist

Medicina. *Meh-de-thee'-nah.* Medicine

Medida. *Meh-dee'-dah.* Measure

Mendigo. *Men-dee'-goh.* Beggar

Mensaje. *Men-sah'-heh.* Message

Mentira. *Men-tee'-rah.* Lie

Mercado. *Mer-cah'-doh.* Market

Metal. *Meh-tahl'.* Metal

Meter. *Meh-ter'.* Put in

Mezclado. *Meth-clah'-doh.* Mixed

Mezquita. *Meth-kee'-tah.* Mosque

Miedo. *Me-eh'-doh.* Fear

Miel. *Me-el'.* Honey

Miembro. *Me-em'-broh.* Member

Mirar. *Me-rar'.* Look

Misa. *Mee'-sah.* Mass

Misionero. *Me-se-au-neh'-roh.* Missionary

Mochila. *Mau-chee'-lah.* Haversack

Moda. *Mau'-dah.* Fashion

Modista. *Mau-dees'-tah.* Dressmaker

Mojado. *Mau-hah'-doh.* Wet

Molécula. *Mau-leh'-coo-lah.* Molecule

Molestar. *Mau-les-tar'.* Bother

Molestia. *Mau-les'-te-ah.* Bother

Mono. *Mau'-noh.* Monkey

Montaña. *Maun-tah'-nyah.* Mountain

Monte. *Maun'-teh.* Mount

Montura. *Maun-too'-rah.* Saddle

Monumento. *Mau-noo-men'-toh.* Monument

Mordisco. *Maur-dees'-coh.* Bite

Morir. *Mau-reer'.* Die

Mosaico. *Mau-sah'-e-coh.* Mosaic

Mosca. *Maus'-cah.* Fly

Mostaza. *Maus-tah'-thah.* Mustard

Mostrador. *Maus-trah-daur'.* Counter

Muchacha. *Moo-chah'-chah.* Girl

Muchacho. *Moo-chah'-choh.* Boy

Mueble. *Moo-eh'-bleh.* Furniture

Muela. *Moo-eh'-lah.* Tooth

Muelle. *Moo-eh'-lyeh.* Pier

Muerto. *Moo-er'-toh.* Dead

Mujer. *Moo-her'.* Woman

Multa. *Mool'-tah.* Fine

Mundo. *Moon'-doh.* World

Muñeca. *Moo-nyeh'-cah.* Doll

Músculo. *Moos'-coo-loh.* Muscle

Músico. *Moo'-se-coh.* Musician

Nácar. *Nah'-car.* Mother of pearl

Nacarado. *Nah-cah-rah'-doh.* Pearly

Nacer. *Nah-ther'.* To be born

Nada. *Nah'-dah.* Nothing

Nadar. *Nah-dar'.* Swim

Naipe. *Nah'-e-peh.* Card

Nativo. *Nah-tee'-voh.* Native

Naturaleza. *Nah-too-rah-leh'-thah.* Nature

184

Náusea. *Nah'-oo-seh-ah.* Nausea

Neceser. *Neh-theh-ser'.* Toilet-case

Necesitar. *Neh-the-se-tar'.* Need

Necio. *Neh'-the-oh.* Stupid

Nefritis. *Neh-free'-tis.* Nephritis

Negar. *Neh-gar'.* Deny

Negocio. *Neh-gau'-the-oh.* Business

Nene. *Neh'-neh.* Baby

Nervio. *Ner'-ve-oh.* Nerve

Neumonía. *Neh-oo-mau-nee'-ah.* Pneumonia

Nevar. *Neh-var'.* Snow

Nevera. *Neh-veh'-rah.* Refrigerator

Niebla. *Ne-eh'-blah.* Fog

Nieve. *Ne-eh'-veh.* Snow

Nogal. *Nau-gahl'.* Walnut

Norte. *Naur'-teh.* North

Noticias. *Nau-tee'-the-ahs.* News

Novedad. *Nau-veh-dahd'.* Novelty

Novela. *Nau-veh'-lah.* Novel

Novia. *Nau'-ve-ah.* Bride

Nube. *Noo'-beh.* Cloud

Nuez. *Noo-eth'.* Walnut

Numismática. *Noo-mis-mah'-te-cah.* Numismatic

Nunca. *Noon'-cah.* Never

Nupcial. *Noop-the-ahl'.* Nuptial

Oasis. *Au-ah'-sis.* Oasis

Obediencia. *Au-beh-de-en'-the-ah.* Obedience

Obeso. *Au-beh'-soh.* Fat

Objeto. *Aub-heh'-to.* Object

Oblicuo. *Au-blee'-coo-oh.* Oblique

Obsequio. *Aub-seh'-ke-oh.* Gift

Observatorio. *Aub-ser-vah-tau'-re-oh.* Observatory

Obtener. *Aub-teh-ner'.* Obtain; get

Ocasión. *Au-cah-se aun'.* Occasion

Océano. *Au-theh'-ah-noh.* Ocean

Odiar. *Au-de-ar'.* Hate

Oeste. *Au-es'-te.* West

Oír. *Au-eer'.* Hear

Ojal. *Au-hahl'.* Buttonhole

Ojo. *Au'-hoh.* Eye

Ola. *Au'-lah.* Wave

Oler. *Au-ler'.* Smell

Olvidar. *Aul-ve-dar'.* Forget

Onda. *Aun'-dah.* Wave

Óptico. *Aup'-te-coh.* Optician

Opuesto. *Au-poo-es'-toh.* Opposite

Oración. *Au-rah-the-aun'.* Prayer

Oreja. *Au-reh'-hah.* Ear

Orfebre. *Aur-feh'-breh.* Goldsmith

Órgano. *Aur'-gah-noh.* Organ

Orgulloso. *Aur-goo-lyau'-soh.* Proud

Orquídea. *Aur-kee'-deh-ah.* Orchid

Oscuro. *Aus-coo'-roh.* Dark

Oso. *Au'-soh.* Bear

Ostra. *Aus'-trah.* Oyster

Oveja. *Au-veh'-hah.* Sheep

Óxido. *Auc'-se-doh.* Oxide; rust

Oxígeno. *Auc-see'-heh-noh.* Oxygen

Pabellón. *Pah-beh-lyaun'.* Pavilion

Paciencia. *Pah-the-en'-the-ah.* Patience

Paciente. *Pah-the-en'-teh.* Patient

Página. *Pah'-he-nah.* Page

Paja. *Pah'-hah.* Straw

Pájaro. *Pah'-hah-roh.* Bird

Palabra. *Pah-lah'-brah.* Word

Palacio. *Pah-lah'-the-oh.* Palace

Pálido. *Pah'-le-doh.* Pale

Palmera. *Pahl-meh'-rah.* Palm tree

Palo. *Pah'-loh.* Stick

Paloma. *Pah-lau'-mah.* Dove

Pantalón. *Pahn-tah-laun'.* Trousers

Pañuelo. *Pah-nyoo-eh'-loh.* Handkerchief

Papel. *Pah-pel'.* Paper

Paquete. *Pah-keh'-teh.* Package

Paraguas. *Pah-rah'-goo-as.* Umbrella

Paralelo. *Pah-rah-leh'-loh.* Parallel

Parar. *Pah-rar'.* Stop

Parecer. *Pah-reh-ther'.* Seem

Pared. *Pah-red'.* Wall

Pareja. *Pah-reh'-hah.* Pair

Pasaje. *Pah-sah'-heh.* Passage

Pasaporte. *Pah-sah-paur'-teh.* Passport

Pasillo. *Pah-see'-lyoh.* Corridor

Pastelería. *Pas-teh-leh-ree'-ah.* Pastry

Pastilla. *Pas-tee'-lyah.* Pill

Patio. *Pah'-te-oh.* Court

Patrulla. *Pah-troo'-lyah.* Patrol

Paz. *Path.* Peace

Peaje. *Peh-ah'-heh.* Toll

Peatón. *Peh-ah-taun'.* Pedestrian

Pedrería. *Peh-dreh-ree'-ah.* Jewelry

Peine. *Peh'-e-neh.* Comb

Película. *Peh-lee'-coo-lah.* Film

Peligro. *Peh-lee'-groh.* Danger

Pendientes. *Pen-de-en'-tes.* Earrings

Penitencia. *Peh-ne-ten'-the-ah.* Penitence

Pensar. *Pen-sar'.* Think

Pensión. *Pen-se-aun'.* Boarding-house

Percha. *Per'-chah.* Coat-hanger

Perdido. *Per-dee'-doh.* Lost

Peregrino. *Peh-reh-gree'-noh.* Pilgrim

Perejil. *Peh-reh-heel'.* Parsley

Perezoso. *Peh-reh-thau'-soh.* Lazy

Perla. *Per'-lah.* Pearl

Permanecer. *Per-mah-neh-ther'.* Remain

Permitir. *Per-me-teer'.* Allow

Perro. *Per'-roh.* Dog

Persiana. *Per-se-ah'-nah.* Shutter

Pertenecer. *Per-teh-neh-ther'.* Belong

Petróleo. *Peh-trau'-leh-oh.* Oil

Picadura. *Pe-cah-doo'-rah.* Sting

Piedra. *Pe-eh'-drah.* Stone

Pijama. *Pe-hah'-mah.* Pajamas

Pila. *Pee'-lah.* Battery

Píldora. *Peel'-dau-rah.* Pill

Piloto. *Pe-lau'-toh.* Pilot

Pimienta. *Pe-me-en'-tah.* Pepper

Pintura. *Pin-too'-rah.* Painting

Piscina. *Pis-thee'-nah.* Pool

Piso. *Pee'-soh.* Floor

Pistola. *Pis-tau'-lah.* Pistol

Plancha. *Plahn'-chah.* (Pressing-) iron

Plata. *Plah'-tah.* Silver

Playa. *Plah'-yah.* Beach

Plaza. *Plah'-thah.* Square

Plomo. *Plau'-moh.* Lead; fuse

Pluma. *Ploo'-mah.* Pen

Pobre. *Pau'-breh.* Poor

Poco. *Pau'-coh.* Little

Poema. *Pau-eh'-mah.* Poem

Poesía. *Pau-eh-see'-ah.* Poetry

Policía. *Pau-lee-thee'-ah.* Policeman

Polvo. *Paul'-voh.* Powder; dust

Pollo. *Pau'-lyoh.* Chicken

Pomada. *Pau-mah'-dah.* Cream

Porcelana. *Paur-the-lah'-nah.* China

Portero. *Paur-teh'-roh.* Doorman

Prado. *Prah'-doh.* Meadow

Precioso. *Preh-the-au'-soh.* Precious

Premio. *Preh'-me-oh.* Prizer

Preso. *Preh'-soh.* Prisoner

Probar. *Prau-bar'.* Try; taste

Profesor. *Prau-feh-saur'.* Teacher

Profundo. *Prau-foon'-doh.* Deep

Prohibido. *Prau-e-bee'-doh.* Forbidden

Protección. *Prau-tec-the-aun'.* Protection

Provincia. *Prau-veen'-the-ah.* Province

Próximo. *Prauc'-se-moh.* Next

Puente. *Poo-en'-teh.* Bridge

Puerta. *Poo-er'-tah.* Door

Pulmón. *Pool-maun'.* Lung

Pulsera. *Pool'-seh'-rah.* Bracelet

Puro. *Poo'-roh.* Pure

Quemadura. *Keh-mah-doo'-rah.* Burn

Quemar. *Keh-mar'.* Burn (verb)

Querer. *Keh-rer'.* Will, want, wish; love

Quirófano. *Ke-rau'-fah-noh.* Operating theatre

Quirúrgico. *Ke-roor'-he-coh.* Surgical

Quitamanchas. *Kee-tah-mahn'-chas.* Stain remover

Quitar. *Ke-tar'.* Remove

Rábano. *Rah'-bah-noh.* Radish

Rabia. *Rah'-be-ah.* Rage

Radiactividad. *Rah-de-ahc-te-ve-dahd'.* Radioactivity

Rana. *Rah'-nah.* Frog

Rápidamente. *Rah-pe-dah-men'-teh.* Quickly

Raro. *Rah'-roh.* Unusual

Rascacielos. *Ras-cah-the-eh'-lohs.* Skyscraper

Rasguño. *Ras-goo'-nyoh.* Scratch

Rata. *Rah'-tah.* Rat

Ratón. *Rah-taun'.* Mouse

Rayo. *Rah'-yoh.* Ray

Rayos X. *Rah'-yohs eh'-kis.* X-Rays

Raza. *Rah'-thah.* Race

Razón. *Rah-thaun'.* Reason

Rebaja. *Reh-bah'-hah.* Discount

Recado. *Reh-cah'-doh.* Message

187

Receta. *Reh-theh'-tah.* Prescription

Recibir. *Reh-the-beer'.* Receive

Recibo. *Reh-thee'-boh.* Receive

Recobrar. *Reh-cau-brar'.* Recover

Recoger. *Reh-cau-her'.* Pick up; collect

Reconciliar. *Reh-caun-the-le-ar'.* Reconcile

Recordar. *Reh-caur-dar'.* Remember

Recuerdo. *Reh-coo-er'-doh.* Souvenir

Red. *Red.* Net

Redondo. *Reh-daun'-doh.* Round

Reembolso. *Reh-em-baul'-soh.* Refund

Refresco. *Reh-fres'-coh.* Refreshment

Regalo. *Reh-gah'-loh.* Present

Régimen. *Reh'-he-men.* Regimen

Región. *Reh-he-aun'.* Region

Reglamento. *Reh-glah-men'-toh.* Regulation

Rehusar. *Reh-oo-sar'.* Refuse

Reina. *Rei'-nah.* Queen

Reír. *Reh-eer'.* Laugh

Relámpago. *Reh-lahm'-pah-goh.* Flash

Remolacha. *Reh-mau-lah'-chah.* Beetroot

Remolcar. *Reh-maul-car'.* Tow

Repetir. *Reh-peh-teer'.* Repeat

Reportero. *Reh-paur-teh'-roh.* Reporter

Representante. *Reh-preh-sen-tahn'-teh.* Representative

Resbaladizo. *Res-bah-lah-dee'-thoh.* Slippery

Resfriado. *Res-fre-ah'-doh.* Cold

Residente. *Reh-se-den'-teh.* Resident

Respiración. *Res-pe-rah-the-aun'.* Breath

Respirar. *Res-pe-rar'.* Breathe

Responder. *Res-paun-der'.* Answer; reply

Responsabilidad. *Res-paun-sah-be-le-dahd'.* Responsibility

Respuesta. *Res-poo-es'-tah.* Reply; answer

Retrato. *Reh-trah'-toh.* Picture

Revelar. *Reh-veh-lar'.* Reveal; (photos) develop

Revisor. *Reh-ve-saur'.* Ticket inspector

Revista. *Reh-vees'-tah.* Review

Rey. *Re'-e.* King

Rico. *Ree'-coh.* Rich

Río. *Ree'-oh.* River

Risa. *Ree'-sah.* Laugh

Rizador. *Re-thah-daur'.* Curling iron

Robo. *Rau'-boh.* Theft

Roca. *Rau'-cah.* Rock

Rodilla. *Rau-dee'-lyah.* Knee

Rompeolas. *Raum-peh-au'-las.* Breakwater

Romper. *Raum-per'.* Break

Ropa. *Rau'-pah.* Clothing

Roto. *Rau'-toh.* Broken

Rubí. *Roo-bee'.* Ruby

Rubio. *Roo'-be-oh.* Blond

Rueda. *Roo-eh'-dah.* Wheel

Ruido. *Roo-ee'-doh.* Noise

Ruidoso. *Roo-e-dau'-soh.* Noisy

Ruina. *Roo-ee'-nah.* Ruin

Rulo. *Roo'-loh.* Roller

Rusia. *Roo'-se-ah.* Russia
Ruso. *Roo'-soh.* Russian
Ruta. *Roo'-tah.* Track

Sábana. *Sah'-bah-nah.* Sheet
Saber. *Sah-ber'.* Know
Sabio. *Sah'-be-oh.* Wise
Sabor. *Sah-baur'.* Flavour
Sacar. *Sah-car'.* Pull out
Sacerdote. *Sah-ther-dau'-teh.* Priest
Sal. *Sahl.* Salt
Sala de espera. *Sah'-lah deh es-peh'-rah.* Waiting-room
Salchicha. *Sahl-chee'-chah.* Sausage
Salir. *Sah-leer'.* Go out
Salsa. *Sahl'-sah.* Sauce
Saltar. *Sahl-tar'.* Jump
Salud. *Sah-lood'.* Health
Saludo. *Sah-loo'-doh.* Regard
Salvaje. *Sahl-vah'-heh.* Wild
Salvavidas. *Sahl-vah-vee'-das.* Life-jacket
Sangre. *Sahn'-greh.* Blood
Sartén. *Sar-ten'.* Frying pan
Sastre. *Sas'-treh.* Tailor
Seco. *Seh'-coh.* Dry
Secreto. *Seh-creh'-toh.* Secret
Seda. *Seh'-dah.* Silk
Sedal. *Seh-dahl'.* Fishing line
Seducción. *Seh-dooc-the-aun'.* Seduction
Seguir. *Seh-gheer'.* Follow
Selva. *Sel'-vah.* Jungle
Sello. *Seh'-lyoh.* Stamp
Semana. *Seh-mah'-nah.* Week
Semejante. *Seh-meh-hahn'-teh.* Similar
Sencillo. *Sen-thee'-lyoh.* Easy
Señal. *Seh-nyahl'.* Signal
Señas. *Seh'-nyas.* Address
Ser. *Ser.* Be

Servilleta. *Ser-ve-lyeh'-tah.* Napkin
Servir. *Ser-veer'.* Serve
Seta. *Seh'-tah.* Mushroom
Sidra. *See'-drah.* Cider
Siempre. *Se-em'-preh.* Always
Sierra. *Se-er'-rah.* Saw
Siesta. *Se-es'-tah.* Nap
Siglo. *See'-gloh.* Century
Silencio. *Se-len'-the-oh.* Silence
Silla. *See'-lyah.* Chair
Simpatía. *Sim-pah-tee'-ah.* Sympathy
Sincero. *Sin-theh'-roh.* Sincere
Sobrina. *Sau-bree'-nah.* Niece
Sobrino. *Sau-bree'-noh.* Nephew
Sol. *Saul.* Sun
Soldado. *Saul-dah'-doh.* Soldier
Sólido. *Sau'-le-doh.* Solid
Soltero. *Saul-teh'-roh.* Single
Sombra. *Saum'-brah.* Shade
Sombrero. *Saum-breh'-roh.* Hat
Sonido. *Sau-nee'-doh.* Sound
Sonrisa. *Saun-ree'-sah.* Smile
Sopa. *Sau'-pah.* Soup
Sortija. *Saur-tee'-hah.* Ring
Sostén. *Saus-ten'.* Bra
Súbdito. *Soob'-de-toh.* Subject
Subterráneo. *Soob-ter-rah'-neh-oh.* Underground
Sucio. *Soo'-the-oh.* Dirty
Sudor. *Soo-daur'.* Perspiration
Sueco. *Soo-eh'-coh.* Swedish
Suegra. *Soo-eh'-grah.* Mother-in-law
Suerte. *Soo-er'-teh.* Luck
Suicidio. *Soo-e-the'-de'-oh.* Suicide

189

Suizo. *Soo-ee'-thoh.* Swiss

Sumar. *Soo-mar'.* Add

Sumergir. *Soo-mer-heer'.* Sink

Surtidor. *Soor-te-daur'.* Filling station

Tabaco. *Tah-bah'-coh.* Tobacco

Taberna. *Tah-ber'-nah.* Tavern

Tabique. *Tah-bee'-keh.* Partition wall

Tacón. *Tah-caun'.* Heel

Tacto. *Tahc'-toh.* Touch

Tapa. *Tah'-pah.* Cover

Tardar. *Tar-dar'.* Delay

Tejado. *Teh'-hah'-doh.* Roof

Tela. *Teh'-lah.* Cloth

Telegrama. *Teh-leh-grah'-mah.* Telegram

Tempestad. *Tem-pes-tahd'.* Storm

Temprano. *Tem-prah'-noh.* Early

Tener. *Teh-ner'.* Have

Teñir. *Teh-nyeer'.* Dye

Terapéutica. *The-rah-peh'-oo-te-cah.* Therapeutics

Terciopelo. *Ter-the-au-peh'-loh.* Velvet

Terminar. *Ter-me-nar'.* Finish

Termómetro. *Ter-mau'-meh-troh.* Thermometer

Tetera. *Teh-teh'-rah.* Teapot

Tiburón. *Te-boo-raun'.* Shark

Tiempo. *Te-em'-poh.* Time; weather

Tienda. *Te-en'-dah.* Shop

Tierra. *Te-er'-rah.* Land; earth

Tieso. *Te-eh'-soh.* Stiff

Tijeras. *Te-heh'-ras.* Scissors

Tímido. *Tee'-me-doh.* Timid

Tinta. *Teen'-tah.* Ink

Tipo. *Tee'-poh.* Type

Toalla. *Tau-ah'-lyah.* Towel

Tonto. *Taun'-toh.* Silly

Topógrafo. *Tau-pau'-grah-foh.* Topographer

Tornillo. *Taur-nee'-lyoh.* Screw

Toro. *Tau'-roh.* Bull

Torta. *Taur'-tah.* Cake

Tos. *Taus.* Cough

Tostada. *Taus-tah'-dah.* Toast

Trabajador. *Trah-bah-hah-daur'.* Worker

Trabajar. *Trah-bah-har'.* Work

Traducir. *Trah-doo-theer'.* Translate

Traer. *Trah-er'.* Bring

Traje (for men). *Trah'-heh.* Suit

Traje (for women). *Trah'-heh.* Dress

Trámite. *Trah'-me-teh.* Process

Tranquilo. *Trahn-kee'-loh.* Quiet

Transferir. *Trans-feh-reer'.* Transfer

Transfusión. *Trans-foo-se-aun'.* Transfusion

Trapecio. *Tra-peh'-the-oh.* Trapezium

Tribunal. *Tre-boo-nahl'.* Court

Triste. *Trees'-teh.* Sad

Trolebús. *Trau-leh-boos'.* Trolleybus

Tropical. *Trau-pe-cahl'.* Tropical

Tubería. *Too-beh-ree'-ah.* Piping

Tumba. *Toom'-bah.* Tomb

Túnel. *Too'-nel.* Tunnel

Turco. *Toor'-coh.* Turkish

Úlcera. *Ool'-the-rah.* Ulcer

Urbanidad. *Oor-bah-ne-dahd'.* Courteousness

Urbanización. *Oor-bah-ne-thah-the-aun'.* Urbanization

Usado. *Oo-sah'-doh.* Worn out

Usar. *Oo-sar'.* Use

Útil. *Oo'-teel.* Useful

Uva. *Oo'-vah.* Grape

Vaca. *Vah'-cah.* Cow

Vacaciones. *Vah-cah-the-au'-nes.* Holidays; vacation

Vacío. *Vah-the'-oh.* Empty

Vacuna. *Vah-coo'-nah.* Vaccination

Vacunar. *Vah-coo-nar'.* Vaccinate

Valiente. *Vah-le-en'-teh.* Brave

Valioso. *Vah-le-au'-soh.* Valuable

Válvula. *Val'-voo-lah.* Valve

Vapor. *Vah-paur'.* Steam; ship

Vaso. *Vah'-soh.* Glass

Vecindario. *Ve-thin-dah'-re-oh.* Neighbourhood

Vecino. *Veh-thee'-noh.* Neighbour

Velocidad. *Veh-lau-the-dahd'.* Speed

Vendaje. *Ven-dah'-heh.* Bandage

Vendedor. *Ven-deh-daur'.* Salesman

Vender. *Ven-der'.* Sell

Veneno. *Veh-neh'-noh.* Poison

Ventana. *Ven-tah'-nah.* Window

Ventilador. *Ven-te-lah-daur'.* Fan

Ver. *Ver.* See

Verdad. *Ver-dahd'.* Truth

Verdaderamente. *Ver-dah-deh-rah-men'-teh.* Truly

Vestido. *Ves-tee'-doh.* Dress

Vinagre. *Ve-nah'-greh.* Vinegar

Visado. *Ve-sa'-doh.* Visa

Visita. *Ve-see'-tah.* Visit

Viuda. *Ve-oo'-dah.* Widow

Vivir. *Ve-veer'.* Live

Volante. *Vau-lahn'-teh.* Steering-wheel

Volar. *Vau-lar'.* Fly

Volcar. *Vaul-car'.* Overturn

Voltaje. *Vaul-tah'-heh.* Voltage

Volver. *Vaul-ver'.* Return

Vomitar. *Vau-me-tar'.* Vomit

Voz. *Vauth.* Voice

Vuelo. *Voo-eh'-loh.* Flight

Vuelta. *Voo-el'-tah.* Return

Yacer. *Yah-ther'.* Lie

Yarda. *Yar'-dah.* Yard

Yate. *Yah'-teh.* Yacht

Yegua. *Yeh'-goo-ah.* Mare

Yodo. *Yau'-doh.* Iodine

Yunque. *Yoon'-keh.* Anvil

Zafiro. *Thah-fee'-roh.* Sapphire

Zanahoria. *Thah-nah-au'-re-ah.* Carrot

Zapatilla. *Thah-pah-tee'-lyah.* Slipper

Zarpa. *Thar'-pah.* Paw

Zarpar. *Thar-par'.* Weigh anchor

Zoológico. *Thau-au-lau'-he-coh.* Zoo

Zorro. *Thaur'-roh.* Fox

Zurdo. *Thoor'-doh.* Left-handed

191

ABBREVIATIONS

A.1.	First class.	Primera clase (barcos)
		Por ext.: Primera calidad
Acct. curt.	Account current	Cuenta corriente
Amt.	Amount	Total
Av.	Average	Promedio
B.E.	Bill of Exchange	Letra de cambio
B.L.	Bill of lading	Conocimiento de embarque
C.I.F.	Cost, insurance, freight	Costo, seguro y flete
C/o	Care of	A la atención de
Consols.	Consolidated Funds	Deuda Consolidada
C.W.O.	Cash with order	Pagadero con el pedido
disc.	Discount	Descuento
D.O.	Delivery order	Orden de entrega
Exch.	Exchange	Cambio, bolsa
f.a.a.	Free of all average	Exento de compensación
F.A.S.	Free alongside ship	Franco al costado del buque
F.O.B.	Free on board	Franco a bordo
F.O.R.	Free on rail	Franco sobre vagón
ins.	Insurance	Seguro
Mdse.	Merchandise	Mercancía
o/a.	On account of	Por cuenta de
o/n.%	Per cent	Por ciento
payt.	Payement	Pago
pd.	Paid	Pagado
recd.	Received	Recibido
T.T.	Telegraphic transfer	Giro telegráfico
wt.	Weight	Peso